ESP: BEYOND TIME AND DISTANCE

ESP

Beyond Time and Distance

by

T. C. LETHBRIDGE

THE SCIENTIFIC BOOK CLUB
121 CHARING CROSS ROAD
LONDON W.C.2

First published 1965
by Routledge & Kegan Paul Limited
Broadway House, 68-74 Carter Lane
London, E.C.4

Printed in Great Britain
by Compton Printing Works (London) Ltd
London, N.1

Contents

Figures

Preface

In the summer of 1923, a party, mostly composed of young men from Cambridge who had just taken their degrees, attempted to go to East Greenland in a chartered Norwegian sealing ship, to do some research work in what was at that time a little known piece of country. As it happened, we encountered the heaviest pack-ice for many years and, after dodging about in the lanes between the ice-flows for weeks, we were eventually forced to turn tail and run for the open sea.

This prolonged delay in the middle of the ice, put a strain on our food supplies, which had not been designed for such an eventuality. We lived for much of the time on the meat of polar-bears, which were shot from the deck. I did not like the proceeding, which seemed worse to me than shooting dogs. But a man must eat.

One day an indifferent shot wounded a bear which, roaring terribly, attempted to amble away over the ice. Of course I joined the party which gave chase to it. You cannot leave an animal in pain.

As I was running over the ice-floe, I trod on a rotten patch and fell straight through into the polar sea. At one moment I was running on a solid surface with no thought except how best to round up the bear; at the next I was in an icy death-trap. I do not remember experiencing the slightest fear, but I do recall the indignant surprise. On the four or five other occasions when I have been very nearly drowned, it was much the same, but not so sudden, nor so cold.

Now something of a similar nature has happened to me again. From living a normal life in a three dimensional world, I seem to have suddenly fallen through into one where there are more dimensions. The three dimensional life goes on as usual; but one has to adjust one's thinking to the other. This book is an attempt to describe what appears to be happening.

I am glad to say that I am not alone in the research work, which is telling us such strange things. My wife is in it too and we act as a team. Her balanced judgement is a great help to me. I have also a circle of pen-friends who give us information and encouragement.

Much of what I have to say will seem incredible to those who believe in the apparent completeness of modern study. But there is absolutely nothing to prevent most normal persons from obtaining the same results as we have done. The only real obstruction appears to be mental laziness. The proof of the pudding must always be in the eating and not in the theories of the author of the cookery book. The dogmas of Victorian science will no longer fit. Many of the better scientists know this. We have to cope with something far beyond the limited approach of exact measurement in three dimensions. It may take a revolution in thought to do this. But it has to come.

When people get to the end of this book, if they can be bothered to do so, they will see that all that we are finding out now is not really new. The facts were known to many men, in many lands, and through many ages. It is only during the last 100 years or so that they have become obscured. Men in the Stone Age apparently knew more about the real meaning of life than the most erudite professor of science today. If this is not just as great a shock as falling through a hole into the polar sea, then nothing is. For we were brought up and conditioned to believe that science either knew all the answers, or was just about to find them. It seems clear now that a huge slice of knowledge has been left out. If this book does no more than draw attention to this fact, it will have served its purpose. So now let us get on with it.

T.C.L.

Chapter One

ON a fine evening on 2nd September 1922, I was one of a number of young people, who had been out catching haddocks with hand-lines from the deck of an elegant motor yacht, *Trident*, the property of a whisky distiller. He was a cheerful, friendly man, who had recently been fined a large sum for running spirits into America, which was suffering at that time from prohibition. His boat changed my rather contemptuous ideas on motor yachts, for she was a fine, able vessel. As we turned to run for her anchorage in Loch Snizort (Fig. 1) on the north-west of Skye and the Ascarib Islands fell away astern, the sun began to set behind the Harris hills on the far side of the calm Minch. Somebody remarked 'Let's see if we can see the green ray.' I had never heard of the green ray and neither apparently had any of the company. We were told that it was a beam of green light sent up by the sun at the last moment of its setting. If you could see the green ray, any wish you made would be granted. Anxious heads at once lined the ship's rail, for some of the young men were interested in the girls on board. Judging by the results, one young man at least must have seen the thing. I saw nothing and never have seen the green ray. I do not know whether there is such a phenomenon, but I fancy that there is. If you stare too long at a bright light and then turn your eyes on to something else, you often see a green spot.

This mystic green ray, with its power to grant wishes, has really little to do with this book. But in it we will be trying to investigate phenomena, which might be described as rays and which are just as mysterious. They appear to link science with magic and magic with religion.

1

Fig. 1. Sunset behind the hills of Harris. Drawn from Tote, above Loch Snizort. August 1922. *Trident is*

A generation after the first incident, with the ashes of the old romances long cold and scattered by the wild Minch gales, we were sitting having afternoon tea in our Cambridge drawing-room with the french windows open on to the garden beyond. We were chatting about this and that when suddenly there was a loud buzz and a large object passed over our heads, settling on a plate at the farther end of the room. I got up and walked over to the plate, which hung on the wall in shadow, to see who our visitor was. To my surprise I saw it was a privet hawk-moth, one of our largest insects. It sat on the plate with its wings closed, not quite in the middle, but nearly so. I went rather too close and disturbed the moth. It buzzed out of the window again and flew down the garden. We watched it fly some 25 yards out from the house. Then it turned round a rose-bed and came straight in at the window again, landing on exactly the same spot on the plate. It did not hover; it just went straight to the chosen place.

Privet hawk-moths are not rare, but the behaviour of this one seemed very curious. I did not disturb it again, but noted carefully its position with regard to the pattern on the plate. It remained there quietly all the evening and did not move when the lights were turned on, but in the morning it was gone. I was much puzzled by this performance. Why had the insect flown twice to a particular plate and chosen a particular spot to rest on?

The plate is an old blue and white one, which has been in the family very many years. It is some 14 inches across and elaborately painted. I had thought that it was Chinese, till a friend, who had made a study of such things, told me that it was Korean and of early seventeenth-century date. I had not been greatly interested in it till this incident with the moth took place. Then I looked at it carefully.

On the spot where the moth had settled there was a very small dab of paint slightly lighter in colour than the blue of the plate itself. I could not think why this was there, so I took it off its hook on the wall to examine the back. The plate is mounted, after the manner of plates which are hung on walls, in a ring of wire. This particular wire ring is wound round in a binding of thin bamboo strips. I had forgotten anything I might have once noticed about the back of the plate, but I now saw that it had a crack, which I believe is called a shake, in it. Someone had feared that the plate might break in half and it had been riveted to make it good. The reason for the dab of paint was that one of the rivet holes had been drilled too far through the plate and the point of the rivet had pierced the glaze on the other side. The paint was put on to hide this mistake. The paint was so well chosen that it needed a close look to distinguish it. However, it was very slightly lighter in shade. This was the spot chosen by the moth. It had been able apparently to choose it from a distance of about 25 yards. Why did a little dab of paint have any attraction for the moth? It could hardly have been a question of colour. It was conceivable of course that the insect might have mistaken the plate for a large blue flower, but it hung in shadow and indoors. This did not seem to be a likely solution. The colour of the dab of paint differed so slightly from that of the rest of the surface that, if the moth had made this mistake it would hardly have returned to exactly the same spot twice.

The attraction then did not appear to be the colour. The plate was in shadow and not shining in the sun, so the attraction was not bright light. I could only think that it was the rivet itself which was the cause.

A number of my friends have been keen on moths. I have not been much interested in them myself and have never collected them, although I know many of the larger species. I have watched friends attracting moths to light-traps at night. I know that collectors put out female specimens of certain moths to attract males from a distance. I have even noticed a female emperor moth in the heather on a moor and, when bending down to look at it, observed a male of the same species fly in, right under my nose, and settle beside its mate. I do not think it is known what causes this attraction. Some speak of it as 'radar', others as 'resonance'.

I turned the plate about in my hands looking for a clue. Then a possible answer came into my head. I was really looking at a very simple and primitive electric coil. The rivet was the soft iron core of the coil and the bound wire ring the coil itself. It

Fig. 2. Privet hawk-moth resting on a rivet on a seventeenth-
century Korean blue and white plate. The two fore-legs are
on the rivet

seemed probable that an infinitesimal current would be generated in this coil and the rivet act as a minute magnet. Purely
by chance the force exerted by this coil might be just equal to
that exerted by a female hawk-moth to attract a male. For, if
my inferences from this incident with the plate are correct, this
is what must happen in nature. I feel reasonably certain that
this is the correct answer and that the male emperor moth for
instance experiences a series of minute electrical tinglings from
the electro-magnetic field of the female. To him they might be
quite large and obviously attractive. (Fig. 2.) I recall that I have
on occasion experienced this myself. It is known as a 'thrill'.

5

I now seem to begin to understand why the antennae of many male insects differ so greatly from those of the females of the same species and often remind one of the strange forest of television aerials in a town. They apparently answer the same kind of purpose. The vibrating leaves on the antennae of many male moths strike the eye at once. As the moth turns them this way and that, it may happen that these leaves pick up the radiation, if one may call it this, of a female. Then the male has only to fly down the beam to find his mate. Apparently the male always flies to the female.

But this sex ray is presumably only one of many. It seems certain that the antennae of the *Lamellicornia*, the scarab group of beetles, must be used also for locating dung. How often on a warm summer's evening has one not heard the drone of a big *Geotrupes* going overhead to some distant heap of droppings? Obviously the beetles might have to walk for days without finding any. But they have this 'radar' device, which homes them straight on to their target. I have watched them arrive; sink a little mine shaft; roll up a ball of dung and then manoeuvre it into the hole where it is used as a store of food for the grubs, which hatch out of the eggs laid in it. Here again, as in the case of the plate, it is not like calling to like, but dung calling to beetle, something very different. It is easy to visualize an electro-magnetic attraction over a short distance between male and female of the same species; but not a distant attraction between a beetle and some partially digested grass. Here mystery begins. (See Fig. 8, p. 39.)

It is always said among hunting people that a dog-fox will travel 20 miles to a vixen on heat. Goodness knows there is a terrible noise here in the night on these occasions. Foxes seem to sit in a row on the road outside our window and bark all night to wake us up. I have tried to estimate what is going on. The dog-fox, who gives two yaps at a time, seems to stay on roads and paths, and run along, at about the speed of a cantering horse, barking at 200 yard intervals. The vixen seldom answers. There may be three or more dog-foxes barking, but little comes from their prospective bride. After a few nights of this activity the dog-foxes grow hoarse and husky. 'Oh! dear,' said my wife,

6

on the last occasion, 'they've all lost their voices.' So they had. They must have been worn out running through the night, for several nights on end, and barking every 200 yards. But there seems to have been a recognizable operation in two stages. First the vixen on heat called up prospective mates from a distance and then they, having found her approximate position on some kind of bearing, could not locate her when they arrived within a mile or so of her position. It is rather a tiresome proceeding. There is nothing much in the dog-fox's bark; but the vixen's call is one of the most creepy sounds that you can ever hear in the night. You hear it more when she has young cubs to train, or so I suppose. The grim cry seems to take you right back through the ages to the time when Britain was a trackless wilderness. Then, as darkness fell, men crept into caves, or tents of skin, and lolled around the fire with their weapons handy, listening to the howling of wolves and the roar of the great stags in the interminable woodlands. There is something wicked in the cry of the vixen and evil in her sly face.

However much the fox-hunting fraternity may have exaggerated the distance covered by her prospective mate, I have no doubt he goes a long way. I find it hard to believe that on the stillest night her voice could be heard 5 miles off. Something other than sound-waves draws the dog-fox to her neighbourhood and then she enjoys puzzling him. She knows how to cut off whatever it is, for the first call would bring all the dog-foxes on to her position, and then when she had decided which bark sounds most acceptable she turns it on in his direction. After that all the other males, hoarse and tired, return to their distant earths. The next night there is no sound and the owls resume command of the midnight sky.

If this were the only example of long distance calling, one might think that a fox's ears were especially sensitive and that the vixen's call carries a great distance, even though she does not appear to utter it. But it is not the only example. For instance a Manx sheerwater, a pelagic bird which only comes ashore to breed, was taken from its chick in a burrow on Skomer and released on the other side of the Atlantic. If I remember right, it took her four weeks, endlessly flying over the north Atlantic rollers to return to her baby. This was not as cruel as it sounds. The chicks are fattened up by their mothers to such an extent that they have to starve for a bit before they leave their burrows.

The shearwater is an amazing bird. In the years gone by, when I sometimes used to stay on Skomer with a friend in the abandoned farm in the nesting season, their evening flight was quite astonishing. They came out of their burrows in hundreds and the air seemed to be filled with screaming ghosts, or valkyries. A whirr of wings filled the sky with a humming sound to which was added yells of demon laughter. Anyone uninformed of this performance, on being taken to a shearwater's breeding site, might easily be crazed with fear. The sky seemed to throb and then a ghastly shriek burst out close beside your head.

What calls the shearwater home to its chick and the dog-fox to the vixen? Two or three thousand miles of sea makes nonsense of any idea of ordinary electrical transmission on the tiny scale presumably available to a shearwater chick. 'Telepathy, of course,' some will answer. Very good, but what is telepathy? As this book goes on I hope to show that my wife and I seem able to produce a kind of artificial telepathy. It is something which needs no mechanically produced current. It sounds impossible, but yet it works. Whatever telepathy may be, however, it is surely too much to suppose that a rivet in an old Korean plate can exert a telepathic influence on a privet hawk-moth. This seems to be an accidental relationship between two electromagnetic fields.

Even a superficial interest in animals leads to some study of their behaviour. It is soon realized that they often react to things, which we cannot see. It appears that they have some sense in addition to the five normally appreciated, sight, hearing, smell, taste and touch. Dogs, cats and horses all have this extra sense, but a cat is probably the easiest to observe. A cat never exerts itself unnecessarily; often sleeps here and there in the day-time, and is really a completely wild animal in casual association with mankind. Unlike a dog, it never loses its personality in that of its owner; although it may show some affection and be lonely at times without its friend. It has a world of its own, which is clearly different from the human world, and it has a perverse sense of humour all of a piece with its general behaviour. For instance, it will carefully watch you sitting down and getting comfortable and, when this operation is complete, get up, stretch, yawn prodigiously and ask to be let out of the door. It has manners and often says 'Thank you', when it is let in again. But this is not a dissertation on cats, I want to talk about their sixth sense.

Now, of a winter's evening, with curtains drawn, fire lit and lights on, the cat will attempt to secure the warmest place. Stretched out in front of the fire, it appears as dead to the world as a hare dropped out of a game bag. Suddenly, for no apparent reason, it wakes up in an instant. Sitting bolt upright it moves its head slowly from side to side and a glazed look comes into its eyes. It obviously sees nothing in the room, but is ranging and fixing the position of something outside; as the unknown thing moves, the head of the cat swings with it. When satisfied, it either returns to sleep, asks to go out, or demands food. As far as one can see, the ranging process is not dissimilar to the old way of firing a gun at a moving target, getting a bracket, one shot over and one short. The cat's head turns wide to one side and then wide to the other and finally settles in between. When this goes on, many people believe that the cat is seeing ghosts. This is not usually the case. Here is an observed example of the proceeding out of doors:

This house, Hole, in Branscombe, stands on the side of a combe, which is narrow and steep sided. The farm on the opposite side is almost exactly 300 yards away and between the two houses the ground falls some 200 feet. Like most of the houses in sight, these two stand on a ledge, or terrace, at the 300 foot level. Between Hole and the slope is a narrow strip of garden bounded by a high wall, which was once the back of cow sheds. I have cut this wall into wide scallops, so that we can lean over it and look at the view. There is a cross wall running back towards the house at right-angles to the scalloped one and almost in the angle I have set a stone seat made from a slate slab taken from a disused dairy. The level of this seat is well below that of the lowest curve in the other wall.

When we are looking out over this curve, my wife's cat

9

invariably materializes and joins in the proceedings. It is seldom visible when we begin to look out, but arrives within a minute or two.

One warm evening last autumn, my wife and I went to look over the wall for a few minutes. The cat appeared as usual, but soon lost interest and went to lie on the seat, which was still in sunlight. Suddenly we saw him spring awake and sit bolt upright. In this position his head was about a foot below the curve of the wall. He could not see out over the curve on which we were leaning. He began his range-finding operation and soon his head became almost stationary in one position. He was not facing directly at the wall, but at a slight angle to it.

Wishing to see what had attracted the cat's attention, we took a rough bearing and looked out at the opposite side of the combe. We saw a small black and white object moving here and there among the bramble bushes about 450 yards from us. We fetched the field-glasses and saw that it was a black and white cat hunting. Had there not been a lot of white on its body, we probably would not have seen it. I do not think we could have noticed a rabbit at that distance. Our cat certainly could not have seen it through a stone wall 2 feet thick. Yet he had sensed it was there. It had woken him up and when he had learnt all he wanted to know he lay down and went to sleep again.

Cats when hunting are remarkably silent. It seems impossible for our cat to have heard the other at 450 yards. One wonders whether some extra excitement on the part of the other cat caused a slight shock to ours and woke him up. Are a cat's whiskers, for instance, sensitive to this kind of thing and do they act like the rod in the hands of a water-diviner? Good water-diviners can sense water by the tingling of their fingertips and have no need to use a rod at all. Good healers are said also to be able to diagnose with no mechanical aids. I need a rod, or a pendulum, for any kind of dowsing, of which water-divining is a part; but at times I do feel a tingling in my fingertips. This is very slight, but resembles the sensation you get if you test the terminals of a small electric battery with your tongue. It is clearly a very small electric shock. From the way he sometimes screws up his mouth, I suspect that our cat gets small electric shocks through his whiskers. This could be tested, I suppose, but it would require considerable ingenuity to perform the experiment.

I have now, I think, given enough examples of this kind of thing to produce a very strong suggestion that insects, birds, foxes, cats and even man himself have some kind of direction-finding apparatus, which is not recognized among the normal functions of the brain. It appears to be a sixth sense.

Chapter Two

I AM now going to try to describe some of our work in attempting to learn about this sixth sense. We have been carrying out experiments for a number of years and these do not seem to have been entirely fruitless. In fact we really do appear to have advanced a little way in this study, which is fascinating because of its very intangibility. Curiosity was frowned upon when I was a child. But curiosity is the foundation of all science. Some seek security, but I thrive on curiosity. What is at the end of that unnamed fjord in Baffin Land, with the gigantic ice-crowned cliffs on either hand? (Fig. 3.) Why did prehistoric man live at a particular spot and what did he do there? What are those little birds fussing about at the edge of the tide? How is that crab going to get out of its skin? My life is made up of innumerable question marks; but I think this sixth sense is the most intriguing of them all.

In my last book, *Ghost and Divining-Rod*, I described our earlier efforts in this investigation and explained the method of using the Dowser's instruments, the pendulum and the diving-rod; but I fear I must go back over a lot of this old ground again in order to make this further study comprehensible. Before I do so, however, I must make one point clear. Despite the sage advice of critics, I am deliberately avoiding the study of the works of others in this line. There is a very good reason for this. It is not known how much thought, conscious or unconscious, may not influence the results which we appear to obtain. If you know what others think the results ought to be, your thought may then influence your own results. We are dealing with a subject which is remarkably intangible. It was a branch of this

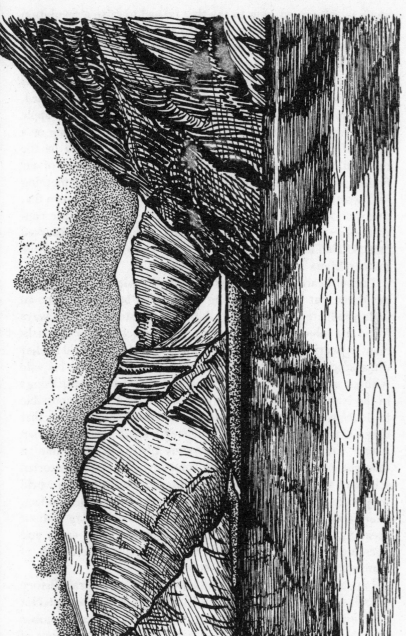

Fig. 3. Two lakes, subsequently named after me, which we found at the end of an unexplored fjord in Baffin land. The summits are about 3,000 feet high. Drawn 1st August 1937. Lakes full of Arctic char

study which caused Jung to say that he had to raise a revolution before science would look at it. He said, and I have also said, that it is mental laziness and a lack of the scientific approach to neglect it.

All science is based on observation and reasoning from this observation. The observation may be incorrectly interpreted, but without observation there can be no science. Newton's apple was an observed fact. So was our privet hawk-moth landing on a plate. If some of our observations could be shown to be the result of our own thoughts reacting on the nerve-endings of our fingers as we hold a pendulum, this would be in itself something well worthy of investigation. However, it will be easily seen that this cannot be the right answer. Thought cannot produce concrete objects out of nothing. This we can do and it is observed fact. So also is the journey of the dog-fox to the vixen and the mother Manx shearwater to its chick.

I never heard of such things as telepathy when a child, and do not think that I knew anything about them before I became an undergraduate at Cambridge. But since that time I have always found the subject very interesting. I can remember my astonishment at hearing an extremely tough and hard-headed old soldier remarking that he frequently communicated thoughts to his wife without speaking. Why was I not being taught about such things in the Natural Science schools at Cambridge? It was impossible to doubt what the old man said. The answer was of course that they did not come within the restricted bounds, which Victorian science had set itself. They were conveniently ignored, like an indecent joke made in the wrong company. And to the Victorian school of scientist they were indecent. To the Darwinian world they were impossible superstition. Yet they were observed fact. Thousands of people communicated thoughts every day without speaking. There is no need to try to prove it by cards and guessing games. It is as well known to the general run of humanity as that they have to breathe to live.

I am afraid I was terribly disillusioned by the Natural History schools of Cambridge. For years I had taken an intense interest in living animals and risked my neck times without number scrambling on dangerous cliff ledges to watch the behaviour of

14

some bird or other. I had observed the wild red deer deep in the scrub oak woods on the edge of the sea in Devon, or on the mountain slopes in Scotland. But now I was expected to reduce the dead bodies of friends to minute fragments to see how they worked. Life had gone: this was mechanics. I have seen precisely the same attitude when training men for war. Outwitting the enemy, by thinking what he will do, appealed to relatively few. What they really liked was to be given a machine-gun and allowed to take it completely to pieces and put it together again so that it still worked. The firing of the gun, so that it hit the target, meant much less to the gunner.

Times have changed since the 20's and people now observe the behaviour of animals without feeling that they must cut them up before doing so. But it still requires one of Jung's revolutions to persuade the scientifically trained observer that there is a sixth sense; that the bulk of humanity knows that there is one and that the secret of life will never be revealed to those who do not appreciate this fact.

Being disgusted with Natural Science, which was my first great interest, I took up archaeology, which had not at that time become so formalized and wooden as it is today. Its leaders were passionately keen investigators, with a great sense of the human side of their problems. Controlled imagination was the key they used to unlock the doors. After years of work on the problems of the two Dark Ages on either side of the Roman period in Britain, I became involved in a study of the early gods of the country. This led to an investigation of the causes of religious belief. Rightly, or wrongly, it seemed to me that these were bound up with the frequent observation of supranormal happenings. People saw ghosts and assumed them to be entities of a higher order from another world. To investigate ghosts I was led to the study of dowsing, water-divining and so on and so back to an investigation of the sixth sense.

It is really all part of one subject. There can be little difference between the manner in which one cat senses another at a long distance and that in which a gipsy senses the winner of the 'Oaks'. Both are distinct from the normal functioning of the brain. But both, as observed fact, do take place. As I described

15

in *Ghost and Divining-Rod*, I have done this myself. I have sensed the winner of a race and the information was communicated to me several hours before the race was won. The means of communication appeared to be a minute electric shock. But this, although it seems to be in accordance with what happened to the hawk-moth and the plate, does not tell you where the information came from. It does, however, apparently tell us, as was observed by Jung, that something about us is independent of earthly time. Clearly the normal functioning of my brain could not have told me what horse would win the Grand National in six hours' time. I am not interested in horse-racing. I do not read the names of horses in the papers. Nothing in my head could have acted as a computer and drawn the answer from the sum of the possibilities. In fact the effect came before the cause, which is blue ruin to orthodox thinking. Yet, judging by the very large numbers of letters which I get from strangers, this kind of thing happens every day. It is observed fact. It is no use dissecting hundreds of brains and finding that thoughts are communicated by tiny electric shocks. These particular shocks happen hours before theoretically they ought to do so.

To form an opinion about such things you must be both your own guinea pig and observer of its behaviour. Only when you have done this for some considerable time can you possibly form an opinion of what is happening to other people. This was the essence of Jung's life study.

Both my wife and myself on occasion receive information about future events, which cannot be obtained by reasoning, or any known functioning of the brain. How could my wife possibly have known where bombs were going to fall near a house in six months' time? She probably got the result telepathically from me who actually saw the occurrence, but nevertheless it was months in advance of the actual happening. According to Jung this is the work of the psyche, or unconscious. I think that it is distinct from the brain and that the means of communication between the supposed psyche and the brain are electrical. To attempt to learn something about all this, we began to investigate dowsing.

Probably all country people and many others besides know

16

something about dowsing. The simplest and most widespread form of this is water-divining. There are few villages which have no one who can find water with a hazel twig and even respectable local bodies sometimes employ a professional dowser before sinking a well. Recently articles from America appear to show that people there are just beginning to notice that there are men employed by large business undertakings to locate water by this means. Years ago, after the marriage of two young archaeologists, I had a letter from a friend, who said, 'I do not think that ye young archaeological brides and bridegrooms understand ye olde English facts of life.' It seems rather like that with modern men. They are so up to date and technical that they have overlooked an obvious piece of knowledge.

My wife and I are quite good dowsers with the hazel twig and regard it now as a rather primitive way of obtaining information. The water-diviner, by this means, finds something which cannot always be readily located by using the ordinary five senses. For water is liable to play curious tricks and frequently does not run where knowledge of geology and topography would suggest. However much the idea may be anathema to some people, still one can find a hidden pipe, or a lost spring, within a foot or so. This is observed fact. It is scientific fact, because the same experiment can be repeated again and again which is the essence of scientific experiment. One can trace the whole length of a pipe and dig it up anywhere along its course to show that it is there. Though its origin is lost in the fog of antiquity; still water-divining must be regarded as an attribute of the human make-up. But here the question of thought comes in. Some people appear to be unable to divine water. It seems probable that either their bodily voltage is too low to work the indicator, or that something in their mentality jams the function. If your whole memory of past instruction tells you that water-divining is an impossibility, this may be enough to prevent your doing it. In some cases too memory may inform the brain that this is magic and therefore wrong; then the nerve-endings in the fingers, which hold the twig, may be automatically told not to react to the stimulus. For the twig is only an indicator of the sensations which are felt by the nerve-endings. As

17

I said before, good dowsers can feel water by the tingling of their finger-tips.

So here again we have something which the brain by means of its five senses cannot know. The information only comes to it by observing the turning of the twig under an influence which does know the answer and communicates it to the nerve-endings of the fingers. If you say that this is the sense of touch, how can you touch water deep under the soil?

Although this influence may well be Jung's psyche, it seems unlikely that it is unconscious. In fact it appears to be very much awake and much more knowledgeable than the brain. It seems to be informed about matters which have not yet taken place, and what goes on beneath the blanket of soil. We will hear more about this shortly.

A divining-rod, it is in reality a fork held in both hands with the point away from the body, is probably the best instrument to use when looking for water and can be made more refined in various ways. It is, however, hardly possible to use it as an instrument of precision. For real study a pendulum is far easier to observe. It seems of little importance what the weight of the pendulum is made of. I have in fact heard it said that a lump of chewing-gum works perfectly well. Personally I use a small ball of hazel-wood, cut from the end of a walking-stick, about an inch in diameter. This has 2 yards of cotton pegged into it with a match stick. The end of the cotton is wound round a 3-inch wooden rod, which can be rotated between the forefinger and thumb of the right hand and acts as a tiny windlass. There are far more elaborate types of pendulum on sale and advertised in the various papers devoted to psychic subjects. Some have cavities in them to include specimens of the objects sought for, magnets and so on. I have as yet found no need for any of these trimmings. My rough hazel ball has so far told me all I want to know. I have made at least two dozen of them for friends and so far everybody has been able to get some results from them. But perhaps it should be noted that young people are often better at dowsing than their elders. They either have more current to spare, or are less constricted by their thoughts.

The method of using the pendulum is to swing it very gently

18

backwards and forwards from the windlass held in the right hand. If a short length of some 3 inches of cotton is used, it will indicate some kind of attraction, or repulsion, between two objects. Or it will show the same thing between the dowser and a single object. Attraction is indicated by the continuance, or increase, of the back and forth movement, oscillation. Repulsion is shown by a deviation from the direct path of the swing and, in my case, by a complete circular movement, a gyration. This 'short pendulum' as I call it, is used by practitioners to tell what pills, food, or drinks are good for people. In practice it seems to tell the truth. For instance, on preparing a lobster for table, I removed what I believed to be the poisonous parts, the brain and digestive tract. The pendulum went into a gyration for these portions and maintained its oscillation for the rest of the meat. Frenchmen are, it seems, often to be seen testing their meals with a pendulum in a restaurant. Ridiculous as this proceeding appears, yet it seems to work.

The implications are very considerable. If the pendulum can really give you this information, not only is it a remarkable safeguard, but where does it obtain its information?

I will go on with this series of observations on the pendulum soon, but before doing so I think it is useful to look at the reactions of others to anything unexpected. Having been brought up to believe what people said, I have taken some time to realize that such credulity is less common than anyone might think. Very many people, especially trained scientists, appear most unwilling to believe anything they do not experience themselves. But the reaction varies very much. I will tell some examples of this kind of thing to show how much belief in various reports can vary.

As an undergraduate, I was interested in early palaeolithic flint implements. These were known to occur on heaps of gravel in a pit on the university farm at Cambridge. Nobody apparently looked for them in the face of the pit itself, but it was important to know which stratum of gravel they came from. I went to the pit, found a hand-axe, now called a bi-face, in the side of the pit and reported it to the Professor of Geology. As he wanted to know the exact place it came from, he came up to the pit where

I found another implement under his nose. Instead of being pleased to see this in the gravel, he immediately thought I had put it there. I had to find another before he recovered.

Years later a similar incident happened with a celebrated bacteriologist. We were walking over the sandy site of a Romano-British village in the Breckland when I asked him not to put his foot down as I had seen the green of a piece of bronze where his foot would have gone. I bent down and pulled a Roman brooch out of the sand. He was furiously angry. He thought I had put it there by sleight of hand. As it turned out, it was the first brooch of this particular type to be found in the country. It was a kind found in the Roman province near the Danube. I could not have planted another specimen, even if I had had the skill to do so.

These two highly trained men evidently went about expecting to be imposed on.

In the summer of 1937 eight of us went ashore at a place we named Turnstone Beach in Ellesmere Land to dig an old Eskimo camp-site. As we were standing by the shore, which still had ice fast to its edge for it was within 700 miles of the North Pole, a puffin bobbed up in the sea close to us. Most of us knew puffins very well and the bird is unmistakable in the summer. On our return to England this was one of the things reported to the professional bird-men. They would not accept it because puffins had not been reported from such a high latitude. But we knew puffins as well or better than they did. It is unlikely that they had fed on them in stews as we did in Jan Mayen in 1921; nor collected the same species of ticks from them as we found on the birds of Skomer, 1,200 miles to the south. However, we were not professional ornithologists, but only physicists, geologists, archaeologists and botanists.

Three years ago a visitor to Beer reported a golden eagle sitting on a post. This was greeted with cries of disbelief. But about a week later a full grown eagle flew up the valley here in bright sunlight and only about 50 yards from where my wife and I were standing. It was being mobbed by herring gulls and its great size was obvious. One could actually see the sun glinting on its beak. This was accepted and published. Incredible as it

Fig. 4. First year golden eagle, drawn 2nd October 1963 from the cliff at Weston, South Devon

may sound eagles do come to this bit of coast and, if not disturbed, would probably remain here. On 2nd October 1963, we saw another, a young one this time (Fig. 4), flop out of the combe at Dunscombe and fly close past us as we sat on Weston cliffs. A cloud of crows, jackdaws and three ravens flew up to mob it. This bird remained in the vicinity till November and we saw it several times. Probably eagles are frequently seen here and come over from eyries in Brittany; but they are confused with the buzzards, which are relatively common and nest in the trees just above the house. As it happens my wife and I have had a lot to do with eagles and know them well. They nested on the cliffs at the west end of Canna and used to hunt the slopes around us when we were digging up in the hills. We have seen them in Argyll, Skye and Assynt and years ago there was an escaped one on Skomer, which you could approach quite closely.

Years ago too I saw an eagle flop over Cambridge. Nobody believed me of course, until it was learnt that it had been hanging about the Norfolk coast and left on the day I saw it. It was probably on its way to western Ireland.

On another occasion I saw a great cross of fire in the frosty Cambridgeshire sky. I knew what it was of course, but again this was not believed until accounts of other sightings appeared in the papers. Perhaps it entitled one to the same benefits as the green ray. In fact I have been rather lucky in seeing fairly rare phenomena. I don't count fog-bows round mastheads, or treble tiers of distant mountains seen in the Arctic; but once, driving northward through Alton in a torrential rainstorm, which slowed my driving down to walking pace, I saw, as I passed a side road, a great ball of fire slowly descending on my left hand side. Unfortunately I was past the turning before it hit the ground and it was far too wet to get out and look. This story was greeted with hoots of incredulous laughter when I got home.

Many things appear in unexpected places when you keep your eyes open. A bittern flies past the window on its way from the Norfolk Broads to the Ouse reed beds. A hoopoe is seen in the middle of a green lane. Black redstarts appear unexpectedly on the roof, or a great grey shrike takes up residence for a day or two in the garden. But, if you are not a professional expert on the subject concerned, the chances are that you will not be believed when you report the happening. The expert very often shows not only disbelief, but annoyance and rudeness. Perhaps the most entertaining case happened in Cambridge. I leant out of a bedroom window and watched a firecrest in an apple-tree below me. I knew firecrests and thought little of it. I did not know that this bird had not been recorded from Cambridgeshire. However, I happened to mention it to a friend, who reported it to an expert. The expert would not accept my observation; but, with incredible naïvety, soon afterwards published a report of his own first sighting of the bird in the district. It would have been terrible for an amateur to have seen it first!

In 1921 I was climbing the southern mountains of Jan Mayen with my late friend Sir James Wordie. We walked up one ridge and unexpectedly saw two giant figures on the next, the Brocken Spectre, silhouettes of ourselves. (Fig. 5.) This to people who had no knowledge of how such things are made would have been monstrous and quite out of this world. But it is not. You can easily make a Brocken Spectre by standing before the headlamps of your car in a fog.

It is hard to see how in a world of this sort anyone believes anything, and no surprise that many scientists go about with a kind of hunted, furtive air. Perhaps it is better to be a geologist. No one can dispute the solid evidence of a fossil, except to say that it must have come from a different bed to the one in which it was found. But even geologists make astounding mistakes Once coming in to anchor under the great cliffs at Wreck Bay on the west of Rum, I was surprised to see that they were of quite different rock to that shown on the geological map. Experts are as liable to error as amateurs. Even the Admiralty chart-makers can err. In Loch Shieldaig an anchor on my chart marked a reef with the sea breaking on it at low water.

So no one must think that what I say about dowsing is fool-proof. To confirm my observations they must test it themselves. But unless they do so their opinions are second-hand. Did I see a great solar cross in the sky, or was it hallucination? Can we be sure that anybody sees what he says that he sees? No, the only person who can know what he sees is the person who sees it, and

Fig. 5. View from the southern end of Jan Mayen. Drawn 21st August 1921, ten days after three of us had climbed the distant Bereneberg for the first time. The Brocken Spectre was seen on the black ridge before the fog

even then he cannot always be sure that he is seeing it with his eyes, or if it is something produced in his brain by the sixth sense. I do not think that you see ghosts with your eyes in the normal way; but I have reasonable proof that ghosts can be seen. Years after I had seen a ghost of a woman in a dark hat with white flowers round it at Hole Mill down below us here, our help produced an old postcard showing the opposite side of the mill with a woman in the same kind of hat, though different clothes, standing in front of it. The woman was certainly not there when I saw the ghost, but she had been there at one time.

As far as material dowsing is concerned, this warning is not necessary. Material dowsing can produce material objects, which can be appreciated by the five ordinary senses. But with the short pendulum and its excursions into the nebulous realm of what likes what, I have as yet no absolute confidence. We will leave the short pendulum for the present and try to see what happens with the long one.

I do not think that the behaviour of the long pendulum has had as much attention given to it as the short. People seem to prefer to use a short one with magnets and all sorts of mechanical aids. But the long pendulum tells you the truth of what is being experienced by the nerve-endings in your fingers. It does not need magnets and samples to tell you this. If you use the long pendulum, you can apparently find the wave-length of anything. You may have to calibrate your own machine, that is to tune it in for your personal voltage; but once this is done the result appears to be infallible. The method is to find the rate, that is the length of cord on the pendulum, which is that of the particular substance you are testing. To find this you hold the pendulum over a sample of this substance, keeping the ball swinging gently backwards and forwards and unrolling the cord. At a given point the pendulum will go into a circular motion. This is the rate for that substance and will be constant for you and your pendulum. The rate is the length of cord between the top of the ball and the bottom of the windlass. If the substance is a metal it will respond to only one rate on the pendulum; but if it is a compound there will be a rate for each element in its composition.

25

Here apparently you have only one source of error. You may not have tuned in exactly. There is nothing except the pendulum between you and the substance tested. With each additional complication, the chances of error increase. Magnets, samples and other aids may help if you have not mastered the idea of tuning in; but to me they seem to be an unnecessary complication. If you were really good at it, you should be able to work with no pendulum at all. The tingling in your finger-tips ought

TABLES OF RATES

I. Material

Rate in inches	Responding substance	Observations
5·5	Phosphorous	
7	Sulphur	
10	Graphite	Reverses the sex rates
12	Carbon	
13	Slate, concrete	
14	Silica, glass and flint	
15	Glaze on pottery	Includes modern porcelain, earthenware, medieval pottery except salt-glaze, Roman 'samian'
21·5	Potassium	An interruptor
22	Silver, lead, calcium, sodium	Lead, sodium and calcium are interruptors. Silver is not. Salt-glaze includes all imported German stone-ware, but not French
22·5	Magnesium	An interruptor
23·5	Vegetable and mineral oils, amber	.
24	Diamond (male principle)	Twice the rate for carbon
25	Aluminium	Earthenware pottery (unglazed)
25·5	Alcohol	All wines and spirits
26·5	Oxygen	Water found on this rate
29	Gold (female principle)	
30	Hydrogen	
30·5	Copper, cobalt	
32	Iron	
32·5	Nickel	Modern coinage

II. Basic

Rate in inches	Responding substance	Observations
9 10 11 }	Light	
20	Life force? Electricity Magnetism slightly longer	All organic material, living or dead. Includes human beings, animals, plants, wood, rubber, coal, paper, bread, potatoes, etc.
24	Male principle	Also diamond
27	Thought, or memory	Most thought is based on memory
29	Female principle	Also gold
30	Sound	Also hydrogen
40	Sleep and death	All dead organic objects. But these also respond to the twenty-inch rate. It seems probable that forty inches represents life force on a higher plane

NOTES TO TABLES

1. It is not proved that these rates are constant for everybody. However, since the rates correspond to the radii of the bases of the biconical fields about the objects studied, it seems probable that, if there is a slight divergence, it can easily be corrected by calibration. The rates certainly are not minutely accurate and have a certain elasticity.

The importance of Table II lies in the evidence it gives of external planning. No accident could have arranged a sequence of 10 inches for the rate of light, 20 inches for the life force, 30 inches for sound and 40 inches for sleep. This must indicate a basic plan. It is also clear that this basic plan includes the dimensions of the human body. An inch derives from the top joint of the thumb, which, although varying slightly in individuals, is an obvious scale for measuring small objects. Had our studies been conducted on the metric scale, it is improbable that we would have ever noticed the basic arrangement.

2. At least one substance seems to have a most disruptive effect on the table. Chalk, which is largely composed of calcium carbonate (calcium 22, carbon 12 and oxygen 26·5) appears to be able to absorb the rates of substances in contact with it and relay the results with a devastating effect on the mentality of the dowser. Strong indications of the existence of buried gold, copper and iron beneath the soil have

proved on examination to have been due to tiny fragments of chalk used in early medieval times to strengthen the clay of a pottery vessel. Practical experiment shows that these rates can be deliberately induced on chalk by direct contact.

to provide the answer. For they are clearly a link between your body and something else.

If you are testing a chemical compound, you will find that it reacts to two or more rates. There is one rate for each element in its composition and these do not mix to give a composite result.

Once you have established a list of rates for some number of common substances, you can analyse specimens whose composition you do not know and find out what they are made of. I include my own table of rates in so far as I have made it out. It may not be exactly the same for every dowser, but it will be in the same order. I hope to show presently why such a variation may take place.

This is only a beginning. It is most interesting to find that the pendulum can be used to locate concealed objects of great variety. If you wish to search for something, which you think may be buried in a given piece of ground, the procedure is as follows:

Tune the pendulum in to the rate of the substance you wish to find and go to the area you wish to search. Set the pendulum swinging at the correct rate from the windlass held between the right thumb and forefinger. Extend the arm and forefinger of the left hand and sweep it slowly backwards and forwards, pointing at the surface of the ground. You stand up and do not move from your position. If the substance you are looking for is indeed beneath the ground, at a certain point the oscillation of the pendulum will begin to change to a circular gyration. You are then in line with the buried object. Mark this line with sticks. Then move to a point somewhere nearly at right-angles and then repeat the process. When a second gyration begins, and you have marked this new line on the ground, you will find that the object is hidden near the point of intersection. It is possible to pin-point the object very exactly. To do this approach the point of intersection with the pendulum swinging. At each point

28

where the oscillation changes to a gyration, put in a peg. It does not take long to plot a circle on the ground. The hidden object will be directly under the centre of this circle. In practice the object can be located within a couple of inches. Nothing appears to be too small to affect the pendulum, although it may be too small to be easily seen with the eye. We have located several tiny brass pins, shoe-lace tags and beads of cobalt blue glass at a depth of 9 inches beneath undisturbed turf.

The pendulum can also be used equally well to analyse a given patch of ground. All you have to do is to mark out the patch, an area with sides 2 feet long is a suitable size, keep the pendulum swinging and note the rate of each gyration. On removing the turf, careful excavation will produce objects of every rate you have recorded. It never seems to fail if you have measured your rates correctly. If there are reactions for glass, copper, iron and so on, when you lift the turf to look for them, the objects will be there. But, like anything else, there are some difficulties. One is that, as can be seen from the table, there are often a number of substances with either exactly the same rate, or one so near that rate that the pendulum cannot distinguish the difference. Another is that some substances are interrupters and prevent the pendulum from responding to the rates of other substances—lead is one of these. If a rate of 22 inches is obtained and a leaden object is dug up, it is then advisable to repeat the analysis for other substances may have been masked. I need not spent more time on this here, for it is described in detail in *Ghost and Divining-Rod*.

A matter of great importance, however, emerges from this experimentation. There is a rate, for me, of 29 inches for gold, but this is also the rate for femininity. There is one of 24 inches for diamond and this is the rate for masculinity. No one could have guessed that the sexes have rates on the pendulum, but they do. Disregarding the fact that it is annoying to find a female beetle when you think you may have located a gold coin, the matter is most remarkable. When I tested the plate on which the hawk-moth had sat, the pendulum immediately responded strongly to the 29 inch female rate. There were also rates of 14 inches for the glaze, 30·5 inches for the cobalt blue of the paint and 32 inches for the iron rivets. Quite by chance then the plate was emitting the female rate, which might be expected to attract a male moth. Unfortunately I was not sufficiently versed in sexing moths to know whether our example was male or female. However, it seems most probable that it was a male and very disillusioned by its experience. This has, however, surely been a benefit to us. Perhaps even insects are often deceived by the vagaries of our peculiar world. It must be so, or so many specimens of male glow-worms would not mistake our bedroom light for the lovely incandescent green shine of the female beetle. Neither would so many specimens of *Aphodius* mistake it for a cow-pat. What the 'red daddy' ichneumons mistake it for I have no idea. Nevertheless it must be rare for a hawk-moth to be deceived by a plate and one moreover which had no gold in its painted design. If it had had this, one could understand that it mistook the 29-inch rate for gold as being the 29 inch for femininity.

Chapter Three

ALTHOUGH it is interesting to be able to go out on one's lawn and to detect, and later dig up, old pins, lost salt spoons, beads, glass, nails and pottery, by magic arts, this is nothing compared with the interest in the problem of why it is possible to perform such a curious action. If everything one found were gold, it would be no more interesting. As it happens the only gold object I found here was an 'Angel' of Edward IV and I got that in the normal archaeological manner with a trowel.

Perhaps I should say that I have done this act of finding buried objects on many occasions and in front of many witnesses. The only complete failure was due to a curious chance. A woman guest ran out into the court and returned triumphantly to say that she had buried a halfpenny and I couldn't find it. No more could I find it, for the simple reason that I tuned the pendulum in for copper (30·5 inches) without realizing that copper coins are made of some alloy which has a rate of 32·5 inches. The perpetrator of this offence went off with a knowing smile thinking that she had exposed the pendulum as being bogus. But she was the only loser. We found a brass pin, a cobalt glass bead and a silver-plated copper spoon with the plating peeling off the copper, under the turf near where she was supposed to have planted the spurious copper coin. There were also several nodules of a copper compound lawn dressing.

To attempt to find out what was happening, I began to work from the known to the unknown. It is known to science that the human body is enclosed in an electro-magnetic field. It is said that the potential of this field is 200 volts; but this, I fancy, is of no importance to our investigation. In practice it is perfectly

31

easy to show that this field exists with a simple hazel twig. For convenience I sometimes speak of this field as a 'psyche-field' to avoid the tedium of the repetition of 'the human electro-magnetic field' or something of that sort.

If you approach a person with the hazel fork pointing at him, it will rotate when the point reaches the edge of his psyche-field. As far as can be observed, this is about 24 inches away from a man and 29 inches from a woman. The force engendered by the meeting of the two psyche-fields is considerable. It is impossible for the dowser holding the fork to prevent it rotating in his hands. In fact I once tried to do so when advancing with the fork on a parson friend. The fork broke off in my hands with a loud crack, causing some surprise and alarm.

You can also demonstrate the existence of the psyche-field perfectly easily with a pendulum. Now the human field is known to exist. This is scientific and well attested fact. It can be demonstrated both by modern laboratory methods and those of a dowser. These two methods may be different, but they are complementary. If one is correct the other is inevitably correct also. There is no way of bilking this. The man who says dowsing is bogus is a mere dogmatist, one of Jung's lazy minds. The facts are there for him to judge and he cannot be bothered to do so.

From the fact that you can detect other people's psyche-fields by the rotation of the twig, or the gyration of the pendulum, it surely follows that when the same kind of thing happens with another object it must be due to a similar cause. The rotation or gyration must be due to the coming in contact of two electro-magnetic fields. The rate of an object is then in a sense its signature and also an indication of its potential. Copper for me will always sign itself at a rate of 30·5 inches and gold at 29 inches. These rates may need calibration according to the potential of the operator, but they will always remain in a constant relationship to each other.

Now, in order to continue our investigation, we must attempt to study these fields. I am well aware that I am not the kind of person to do so. I have not the necessary deep knowledge of physics. Why should an archaeologist have such knowledge?

32

My temerity in doing this investigation is downright impertinence; but the behaviour of those who could do so and cannot take the trouble is worse. It is downright laziness. Well, then, are these fields simple examples of static electricity or is this only a part of the answer? Is it not possible that they are something to do with a much greater force, the life force perhaps, which is not yet explored?

In my ignorance I assumed that the field would surround the object like a skin and be spherical. I imagined a kind of cherry with a stone inside. But very little investigation with the pendulum showed that this idea was quite wrong.

As we worked out a circle on the ground to find a buried object, so we can put a given object on the floor, approach it from several directions with the pendulum swinging and plot the points at which it gyrates. This is the edge of the object's field. It may not be a circle of quite the same size for each operator, for the point of contact may depend on the strength of the dowser's psyche-field. But one thing is constant and appears to be a law. The rate, that is the actual length of cord on the pendulum, necessary to tune in to the object, will always be the same as the radius of the field of force in the horizontal plane around that object.

Now, if the field of force were a sphere, one would have only to repeat the process downwards until you reached the edge of it. But you cannot do this. The field extends upwards, as one can easily test, through the floor of the room above and on up to the ceiling of that room. If you measure and draw it, you appear to be dealing with a very tall cone on a very small base. If you reverse the process and test for the field downstairs with the object up above, you find that there is a second cone of the same size going downwards through the floor. The object is, as I think I have said somewhere before, for all the world like a fly squashed between two ice-cream cornets, mouth to mouth. (Fig. 6.)

I am speaking only of substances with a single rate. In the case of chemical compounds there are two or more sets of double cones inside one another. The radius of the base of each double cone equals the rate for that element on the pendulum.

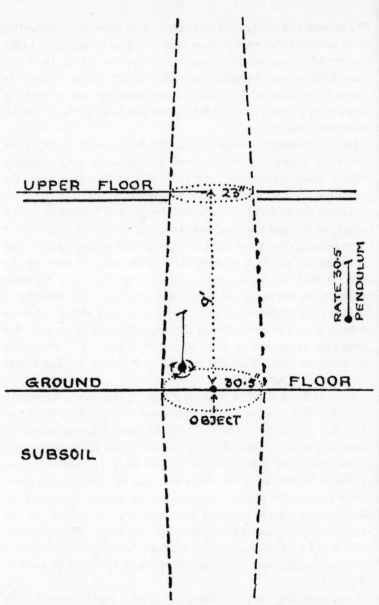

Fig. 6. Simple diagram to show ascertainable portion of the double cone of copper and the relationship between its radius and the rate for the pendulum

This extraordinary situation has not, as far as I am aware, been observed before.

The cones are certainly very high and I have not as yet been able to reach the apex of even the ones with the smallest radius. That for sulphur is only seven inches, but I cannot find the apex of its cone. It seems to me that each cone may in reality be drawn out into a single thin ray. If so the ascending ray probably passes out into space, while the descending one extends to the magnetic centre of the earth. I suspect that we are really dealing with something in the study of Harmonics and that these things resemble the figures formed by plucking taut strings, except that the vibration of a taut string only takes place in one plane, whereas our fields vibrate in all directions. Should there by any sense in my suggestion, one can appreciate two things. The first is that the ascending rays could perhaps come in temporary contact with the fields of the sun, or moon, and secondly they might form paths by which the force of gravitation could travel.

There is another possibility. Since you can with a single pendulum only find one point on the surface of a cone at any one time, there is no means of telling whether the whole cone is always there, or whether it only exists in one plane at one moment. The contact between your psyche-field and the field of the object might be similar to the plucking of the taut string and the conical appearance might be due to a succession of contacts round the perimeter. In other words the apparent cone may be an illusion and all that is really there be a single ray of indefinite extent, agitated into conical form by a series of shock contacts. The way to test this is to have several operators approaching a given object at the same time and each oscillating a pendulum calibrated to their own rate for that substance. We have found by using two pendulums and two operators that the cones appear always in position. From whatever direction they are approached, the result is the same.

As far as this investigation is concerned, it is not of great importance what form the field of the object takes. The important point is that one's own field can discriminate between the infinite and interlocking fields of a variety of substances. It can without hesitation pick out the ascending field of a buried pin, or bead. This is something which none of our five senses can do unaided by elaborate mechanical contrivances. It is what is popularly known as magic; but television is in just the same category. The fields of objects may be cones, or they may be rays of considerable complexity; but, invisible and intangible as they are, we can make contact with them by employing our sixth sense and using a pendulum as an indicator.

Since we have our own fields, composed of a considerable collection of ascending and descending cones, or rays, it seems probable that we may be ourselves influenced by magnetic forces from the moon and even from far distant planets and stars. It is possible that the study of astrology is not so improbable as it might appear. I heard the late Professor Joad once proclaim that 'astrology is bunk', but later he became a professing Christian, accepting many dogmas which seem far more improbable. I can accept most of the facts recorded in the Gospels, there appear to be some interpolations, but I cannot reasonably believe much of the dogmatic theory based on the interpretation of the Gospels. Having spent much of my life trying to disentangle the scanty facts about the Dark Ages and struggling to make sense of the contemporary chronicles, I find it very hard to believe that the interpretation of Christ's teaching, produced by the Christian fathers during that epoch, is likely to bear much relation to what He really taught. I do not know whether astrology is bunk or not, but seeing what Joad would accept, I do not think he was in a position to condemn astrology without deeper study. I cannot be bothered to study its intricacies myself, but I begin to see how it might work. The moon, for instance, is known to pull the oceans and make the tides; vegetable growth has been shown scientifically to be affected by the phases of the moon; although it is scoffed at by many, observers see changes in mental patients as the moon waxes and wanes. It presumably exerts a pull on any fluid and so alters pressures in the human circulatory system. If the moon can exert such an influence, the planets might well do so too. I do not know the answers, but feel it wiser not to scoff at an unstudied subject without proper study. Joad was, I feel, very conceited to do so.

The human field is clearly not restricted to its vertical axis. We have seen that it can be extended by using a pointing finger to search for buried objects. With a view to getting some idea of the range over which this searching can be carried out, I have tried extending it by holding a light cane in the left hand. Although it is difficult to extend one's arm for any length of time and hold the pointer steady, it is clear that the ascending cone of a copper pot can be registered at a distance of 150 yards and that of a sheet of corrugated iron at 300 yards. This is getting near that of the ranging procedure of the cat at 450 yards mentioned above.

After all, this radar-like proceeding is not very unlike what is known to happen with bats. The bats are believed to use their highly specialized ears to send out a beam whose 'echo' returns from any solid object in its path; but who shall say whether it is the solid object which returns the echo or its electro-magnetic field? As it happens Hole is a good place to observe bats. The greater horseshoe bat frequently hangs up from beams in the kitchen and during the summer there is in June a kind of convocation of *Pipistrelles*. As many as 114 of these little bats have been observed in a single evening emerging from a hole beneath a barge-board under the roof.

It is very easy to watch the horseshoe bats (Fig. 7). When hanging up their whole body appears to quiver with great energy. The head swings to one side first up and then down. Then it swings over to the other side and repeats the motion. It is clearly continuously sweeping a hemisphere of kitchen with its beam. The energy required to do so seems to be very great for the size of the animal. The whole operation appears similar to that performed by a *Geotrupes* beetle (Fig. 8), who vibrates all over and changes the direction in which he is facing, until his body points the right way, before taking off from the ground. He has highly specialized antennae, corresponding in a way to the bat's amazingly complicated ears. The target for the bat's ears may be a concrete one, or it may be something only known to us through the pendulum. The target for the beetle can hardly be the actual piece of excrement, more than 100 yards away. It must surely be ranging on one or more of our intangible cones

37

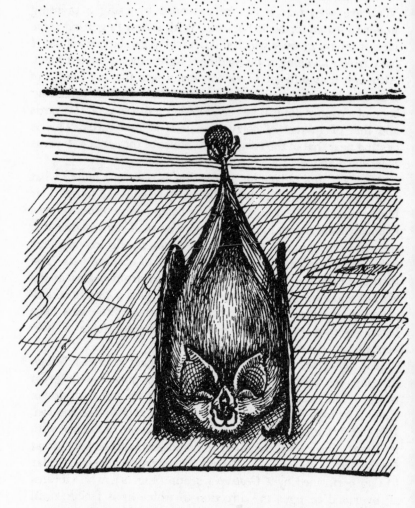

Fig. 7. Sketch of a greater horseshoe bat hanging from a beam
in the kitchen at Hole and using its 'radar'. The body, vibrating
intensely, makes a half-rotation each way. At the same time
the head is first raised, as it is here, and then lowered. The
head is lifted up backwards. This is a view of the back.

(Actual size)

Fig. 8. Sketches of three British beetles which apparently fly
on beams. 1. Dytiscus, marginalis, flies to stagnant water, ♂
2. Geotrupes, pyrenæus ♂ and 3. Geotrupes, typhæus, ♂
which fly to dung. Probably most beetles do this homing flight.

(Actual Size)

surrounding that piece of excrement. It seems probable that the
bat does the same and that in his ears we see a perfect adaptation
to the interpretation of messages from the sixth sense. The bat,
the beetle, the cat, the fox, the moth and the bird can all
apparently utilize something which to us is only recognized

D

directly when somebody is said to have a good 'bump of locality'.

Articles in scientific journals have recently demonstrated the existence of this 'bump of locality' among various small organisms in relation to the earth's electro-magnetic field. The animals which we have glanced at appear to be reacting to much more limited fields than that of the earth, but the idea is the same.

As far as we can observe at present, the distance to which these rays, if that is the right term, can extend is relatively very great. To the cat a distance of 450 yards appears to be nothing. The moth comes in to its mate over unbroken miles of heathery moor. The shearwater flies something like 3,000 miles to its chick. Distance, has, unlike mechanical electricity and magnetism, apparently nothing to do with it all. The power of the transmission ought in theory to decrease in relation to the square of the distance. Our transmissions apparently do not conform to this law. But why should the laws which man has worked out for his mechanical products conform to the rules set by nature? We are probably trying to study an attribute of life itself.

This is becoming an extraordinary and most difficult picture. It seems that our electro-magnetic field and those of animals, can project a ray to an unlimited distance, through a forest of other ascending rays, and will with this single out a particular ray and record it by a gyration of the pendulum. To get any idea of what appears to be happening, we must now go back to the short pendulum for a little.

Take two small objects of the same material and put them a foot or so apart. Do not take a modern penny and an old one, for, as I have said before, they are of different metals. Swing the pendulum between them. It will oscillate as long as you can be bothered to hold it there. There is no obstruction. The pendulum swings freely backwards and forwards. Now substitute an object known to be of a different substance for one of the originals and swing the pendulum again. It swings out of the line between the two objects and with me goes into a complete gyration. Presumably the current, which at first flowed freely

40

between the two objects, has now met an obstruction and can no longer pass freely. But is not this the object of the bat's radar? Things are not observed by affinity, but by the turning back of waves, or rays, or whatever they may be, against an obstruction. This is how our pendulum works. It records an obstruction to the flow of some kind of current between you and what we must presume to be the earth's field. The flow of current could presumably continue unchecked if there were no obstructions. But there always are obstructions and you can identify which they are by tuning in to their own particular rate of vibration.

With the short pendulum you can show apparently what opposes the free flow of current between you and the earth's field. Some substances seem to encourage this flow, others oppose it. This is like nothing in man-made electricity or magnetism. It is far more varied and of wider scope. It is not only apparently intensely selective, but it also appears to be free from the limitation of earthly distance. As we go on I hope to show how it is independent of earthly time also.

Naturally it really needs a great number of trained experimenters to work at this subject; but it is quite surprising how much can be learnt in complete simplicity. Rates can be found by inference, which in theory could only be obtained in a laboratory. For instance gases can yield up their rates by a pendulum analysis of several of their compounds. One seldom has an oxygen cylinder available in a country house, nor the apparatus for separating hydrogen. But the pendulum shows that in a compound the rates for the various chemicals composing it do not merge. Each has its own particular cone of a particular size. Therefore, if you wish to find the rate for oxygen, all you have to do is to take a few of its compounds, their names often end in -ate, and see which unknown rate is common to all of them. By this method it is soon shown that the rate for oxygen is 26·5 inches and that for hydrogen 30 inches. Water thus has two rates 26·5 and 30 and you can test this without difficulty. With the divining-rod you can only find water because it forms an obstruction of some sort.

For instance if you want to obtain the rates for something

like gypsum, calcium sulphate, you have two unknowns which you cannot find by direct observation. Calcium you do not obtain easily and oxygen is a gas. Well, there are several salts of calcium about the place, calcium carbonate for instance, which comes into the composition of every snail shell. By testing these you find a common rate for calcium, which is 22 inches. Carbon is easily found by direct testing of some soot off the fire back; it is 12. By further testing of the sample, you find an unknown rate of 26·5 which you suspect of being oxygen. Then test a few substances which are known to contain oxygen; sulphates, phosphates, chlorates, carbonates and so on. It is soon evident that 26·5 is indeed that rate for oxygen. This dowsing seems to be a ridiculously simple method of chemical analysis. It is very rough and ready as I do it, but it would not be difficult to elaborate it so that minute differences in rates would show accurately on some scale. It might prove a great saving of time and money, but it is not my job to find out the ways and means. I am not interested in the elaboration which must eventually come in this subject, but am only an explorer searching for the main points.

At the very end of *Ghost and Divining-Rod* I mentioned one of these points and it is one which seems to have a most important bearing on a large branch of parapsychology, psychic study. There is no need to sniff at this. Jung was a keen student of parapsychology and so have been several famous scientists. They were all believed to have gone mad of course, but that is the usual reward for anyone who has the courage to step over the fence of orthodoxy. In our own case we may be less unfortunate. Something supposedly occult seems to step into the world of science.

I have mentioned already the calcium salts. Calcium sulphate is the well-known mineral gypsum with its varieties alabaster and selenite. If you take a lump of gypsum straight off the beach here and analyse it with the pendulum, you obtain rates of 22 for calcium, 7 for sulphur, 26·5 for oxygen and 32 for iron which occurs as a trace and colours alabaster red. But suppose, as I sometimes do, I take the lump of gypsum and as it is soft and a nice colour, carve it into the shape of a fish, a horse, a

42

rose, or anything I fancy and then test it again, there is a new rate, 24, added to it. That rate of 24 we know to be the rate for masculinity. Somehow I have added my male signature to the various cones composing that piece of alabaster's field. This inanimate, biconical, field of force has had something alive added to it. This is, in a sense, creation. (Fig. 9.)

From any point of view this is a most astonishing thing. But the men of old knew and primitive tribes today still know it. It is only so-called civilized man who has forgotten it. This is the reason why pagan Anglo-Saxons frequently broke combs of dead people and buried them with their ashes in urns. There was something of the spirit of the dead person in that particularly individual possession, a comb. Nobody wanted to use the comb again for fear of being haunted. Therefore they broke it, killed it, and buried it with its owner. The early Norsemen did just the same with a dead man's weapons. They deliberately broke, bent, or hacked out of shape his sword, spear and shield and buried them in his howe. I was most interested in this point. I knew the evidence and had heard the suggestion of the reason from anthropologists, who had worked among primitive peoples in the East. But in my wildest moments I had never dreamt that there was any valid reason for the belief. Now a ball on a bit of cotton explains that there is something transferred from the owner of an object to the object he owns. All through this investigation we come on instances of apparently absurd primitive ideas being confirmed by the dowser's instruments. Early people knew far more than they are given credit for, because they were much better observers than people are today. They had to be. All through the millennia of prehistoric times a man who was not a good observer had little chance of survival. Some extra faculty in the more natural state of early man informed him of the mana, perhaps we would call it current, of the dead person that had become fixed in association with the things he used and the things he made. But how this was learnt we cannot tell. We can only guess it made itself apparent by a tingling in the finger-tips of the persons who touched the objects.

It is most interesting to expand this study. Paintings, for

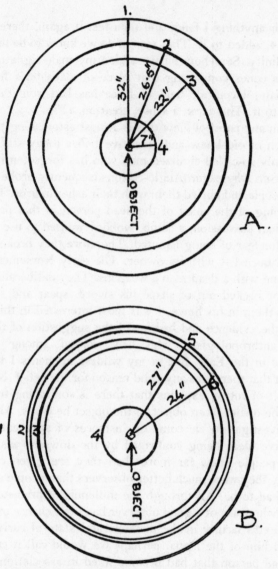

Fig. 9. Pendulum analysis of two pieces of alabaster. A. Untouched. B. Carved into shape by man. 1. Iron (trace). 2. Oxygen. 3. Calcium. 4. Sulphur. 5. Thought. 6. Male. It is clear that two extra rates have been added to B during the carving. (The circles represent the base area of each double cone)

instance, seem to retain the sex of the artist for at least 150 years. I have two miniatures by Shelley above my head as I write this. One is of a soldier, a Captain Gordon in the uniform of the 91st, Argylls. The other is of his niece, Mrs. Masterton, who had the exciting experience of escaping from Toulon when it was taken from the Royalist French by the Revolutionaries. She got away in a British frigate and married one of the officers. You would have thought that this portrait of my very lively looking great-great aunt might have a different sex rate to that of the picture of the soldier, and have reacted to the 29 inch rate for femininity. But it does not and both pictures have the 24 inch male rate, which was presumably painted into them by Shelley.

I have been tested on occasion with unknown pictures by unknown artists and asked to find out whether the painters were men or women. So far I have not had a failure; although at least once I should have judged the opposite if I had not had the pendulum. (Fig. 10.)

This of course explains something which I have never understood before. Why is it that a photographic portrait, however well it is taken, never has the life in it which you appreciate even in a mediocre painting? The answer is that the photographic portrait, beautiful though it may be, is entirely mechanical and has nothing from the photographer himself in it. However, the painting has some gift of life from the artist. It is not from the sitter and, although the picture may look astonishingly alive, that sensation of life which we can appreciate is a detached portion of the psyche-field of the painter himself. If the famous paintings of female nudes from classical times to the present day could come alive, you would not see beautiful women stepping out of the frames, but bearded men with paint smears on their clothes. It would be as sad a disappointment to these artists as it would have been to Pygmalion if Galatea had come alive as a man.

Of course it is most improbable that the sex rate is the only rate implanted by the maker in the field of the object which he makes. If he can impress an object with his sex, surely something of his thought, memory and personality must go with it

45

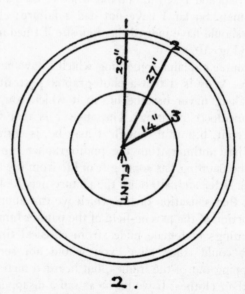

Fig. 10. 1. Flint scraper, probably made about 3,500 years ago, dug up in the garden at Hole and tested at once with the pendulum. 2. Diagram of the rates obtained by this analysis. 1. Female sex. 2. Thought. 3. Flint. Such scrapers are very common and believed to have been used by women for scraping fat off skins

too. I evidently made some wrong deductions when summarizing the results of some experiments in psychometry, which I described a few years ago in *Ghost and Ghoul*. Then I came to the conclusion that nothing could be impressed on the field of an inanimate object and such things only acted as a link between two persons. The pendulum shows clearly that I was wrong. But I am not in the least abashed. One must form one's opinions from the information available at the time. The mistake occurs when these opinions become so rigid that you no longer have the courage to change them. I see clearly now that some part of a personal field can be detached from its owner and attached to another field. I think it is quite clear too that this detached portion remains intimately linked to the main psyche-field of the person involved. As I hope to show presently this has implications, which are wide enough to destroy the whole argument for materialism.

Chapter Four

IF you cut off a lock of your hair, it is then, in theory, dead. It certainly does not live for very long. Take the lock of hair and put it in a sterilized glass bottle. It certainly was grown on your body and in that sense is a part of you. But it is no longer growing and is now dead and isolated. Now, for at least 2,000 years, it has been maintained that a bit of your body, a lock of hair, a finger-nail paring, a drop of blood, or even a gob of spit, remains in contact with the person from whom it originated. Those who practised witchcraft believed that they had only to obtain possession of something of this kind to be able to influence the body of the originator for good or ill. The modern mechanical healers with 'The Box' go entirely on this assumption and in practice it seems to work. They believe that it cannot work for ill; but the older practitioners held otherwise. To do ill by magic, to 'Work Black' as it was called, was always thought to be extremely dangerous to the performer. If anything went wrong, the whole force of the hostile magic returned to him. As it happens I do know at first hand of a case where this seemed to have occurred. A quarrel arose between the magician and a neighbouring farmer. In spite of advice, the magician decided to put a murrain on the farmer's cattle. Something went wrong. The magician died suddenly in circumstances which to many people suggested murder. 'No names, no pack-drill.' In due course the murrain did fall on the cattle. but it fell just beyond the farm of the intended victim. It fell on two farms in a line between the magician and the victim. A line about 100 yards wide includes the house of the magician, the house of the intended victim and the two farms inflicted by the

48

murrain. There the visitation stopped, except for infected animals which had been moved to markets and such-like. This happened a number of years ago. It was hard to take an objective view and to believe that everything was pure chance. The quarrel was violent. The magician had had many years of instruction. The proposed curse was widely known. The disease fell inexplicably in the wrong places. The magician died. This is exactly what should happen in theory. What happened in reality, I do not know and neither does anyone else. To anyone who knew the magician, the coroner's verdict was not convincing and the medical evidence improbable.

Now let us return to our lock of hair shut up in its sterilized bottle. After a week or two it must be completely dead. Then test it with the short pendulum against the body of its former owner. The answer given by the pendulum is an oscillation. Not only is the living body pleased to contact its former possession, it appears to be delighted. The oscillation increases and almost becomes violent. Anyone who can work the pendulum at all can test this and see that I am right. The dead object retains a field and this field is in agreement with the field of the body which grew it. Test the hair in the bottle for sex. It will react to the sex rate of the former owner.

The dead hair reacts to a sex rate. It occurred to me to try to find out how long this rate persisted in a dead object. It seemed most improbable from a materialistic point of view that it could persist at all. The thing is dead and that ought to be the end of the matter. Nothing should remain of the life which once animated it.

I have a pernicious habit of picking up fossils whenever I happen to see them and, having a sharp eye, I find quite a number of them. I bring them home and they lie about on window ledges and so on, collecting dust and spiders, till someone puts them in a box in justifiable indignation. Although I did not expect to get any results, I thought it would be interesting to test a few fossils. On looking round the house I found that I had thirteen specimens of the chalk fossil, *Mieraster cor-anguinum*, which is generally known as 'the shepherd's heart' and down here as 'the heart of the flint'. Twelve of these fossil sea urchins are casts in silica of the inside of the shell, 'test' as it is called. One is the test itself, which I had dug out of the actual chalk. The silica, which formed the casts inside the tests, is said to have been collected from the water of the ocean as the animal inside the shell decayed. How this was done, I do not know; but you could surely not have anything much more dead than these casts of the insides of sea urchins, which, at a rough estimate, perished in the deep water of the Cretaceous Seas some 100 million years ago.

I took these thirteen fossils into the hall and placed them one by one on the slate floor, which is relatively free from interruptions. I tested them in isolation for sex with the long pendulum. Six gave a reaction for the male rate. Five, including the specimen with a real shell gave the female rate and two gave both male and female.

The most astonishing thing about this experiment was that there should be any sex rate, or magnetic rate, or any rate at all except for silica, from the casts of sea urchins which had been dead for such a stupendous length of time.

I had forgotten anything I might once have learnt about the sex life of sea urchins while an undergraduate at Cambridge and did not know whether you could tell a male sea urchin from a female, or whether they might not be hermaphrodite like earth worms. I took the fossils and examined them with care. (Fig. 11.) It was clear at once that there was a great difference between the casts which the pendulum said were female and those it designated as male. The one with the actual shell in place was of course different from both, because one was looking at it outside, while all the others were impressions of the inside of the shell. We will leave it out of the study and deal only with the casts.

In the case of the male casts there is a beautiful five-pointed star on top like a picture of a leaf. This shows what are known as the ambulacral grooves, through which little tube-like feet once projected giving the animal both motive power and a breathing apparatus. The base of each foot is clearly marked on the cast giving an elaborate and attractive pattern. In the case of the casts, which the pendulum calls female, little of this

50

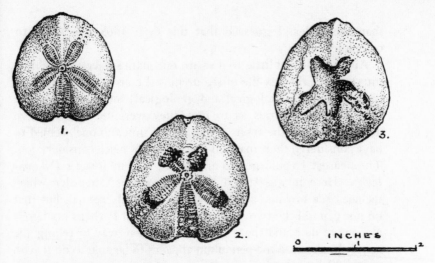

Fig. 11. Cretaceous fossil sea-urchins. Flint casts of the interiors. These give sex rates on the pendulum. 1. Male. 2. Male and Female. 3. Female. Species is Micraster cor-anguinum

pattern remains. The places where the feet used to be are taken by five deep hollows. It was evident to me that when the urchins died there were swellings extending inwards from the ambulacral areas into the body of the animal. These were naturally reproduced in the cast as hollows. The shell above had not gone, but was obscured. It seemed to me that the swellings, which produced the hollows, must have been bunches of eggs. The casts, which gave both male and female reactions on the pendulum, appeared to show that the swellings were just beginning to form. The male pattern had begun to break down and hollows were starting to form on top of the cast. A very small specimen, which I found later, showed little sign of the ambulacral areas and gave no sex reaction at all.

Without knowing more than this, I inferred that this kind of sea urchin began its life without sex. Then it became male. When it had shed its male seed, which in the case of an oyster is known as spat, I assumed that it produced eggs and was then female. When the eggs were fertilized, I presumed that the organism had finished its life cycle and died, for there is no further male stage. The female fossils are roughly a size larger

51

than the males. I guessed that this cycle took two years to complete.

Although it had little to do with our main subject, I was now interested in the sex-life of sea urchins. I consulted a number of handbooks both zoological and geological; but although there were several theories as to how they were thought to have developed down the aeons of geological time, no one seemed to have considered their married life worthy of much consideration. The nearest I could get to an answer was in *Wood's Palaeontology*. Here it was stated that *Echinoderms*, an order which includes sea urchins, are as a whole generally sexual, but that no one can tell the two sexes apart. Ah well! Perhaps my books are out of date and there is now some easy way of telling the sexes. In any case the pendulum appears to be able to do it with no trouble at all.

Now, to return to our lock of hair in its sterilized bottle. It is, of course, dead in the normal sense, but it gives a reaction to the male sex rate. I tried both my living self and the bottle of dead hair opposite the dead casts of the sea urchins. In each case the tests gave the same results. If living male body, or dead male hair is placed opposite a fossil regarded as male by the long pendulum, when the short pendulum is swung between them, a gyration, or disagreement is indicated. When a supposedly female fossil is substituted for the male one an oscillation, or agreement is shown. This was constant and has to be accepted as a fact. Current passes freely between male and female. Between male and male or female and female there is an obstruction. We saw, however, that with inanimate objects current apparently flowed between like and like and was obstructed when the composition of the objects was different.

The very important point which comes out of this simple series of experiments is that some trace of the original sex life remains in fossils after a period of some 100 million years. The original inmate of the fossil shell has been dead all that time and yet a detached portion of his field obviously still remains and can be detected through our own field and our nerve-endings by a pendulum.

Not only is this the case; but a sample of our dead hair is

apparently able to talk with the dead sea urchin. Something must be still alive surely and outside our notion of time.

To find out more about this strange matter and attempt to make sure that I was not exercising thought and influencing the pendulum, I thought out another experiment.

This needed two dowsers in different rooms, each with a pendulum. My wife went upstairs taking with her a pendulum, a male and a female fossil sea urchin and a bottle of my hair. I remained below in the stone-flagged hall, while she conducted her operations over a concrete fireplace in the bedroom. I tuned in my pendulum to the 24 inch male sex rate of my hair in the bottle upstairs. My wife swung the short pendulum between my hair and a fossil sea urchin of which I could not know the sex rate. Watches had been synchronized. At a given moment I began to swing my pendulum in the hall downstairs, while she swung her's in the bedroom.

I am really a terrible disbeliever. I did not for a moment expect a tangible result. However, after a few moments, the pendulum began to oscillate with much greater fervour than usual. Apparently the double 'voltage' had increased its reaction considerably. 'Good heavens!' I thought, 'she must have been trying my hair against a female sea urchin.'

We broke off for three minutes and then I swung the pendulum again. Instantly, and with great violence, it went into a circular swing. It was so strong that I felt a sharp tingling in my finger-tips and could not keep them steady. 'A displeased male,' I thought.

My wife joined me. I had got both answers right. It was perhaps only one answer; although my wife might have tested the same sea urchin twice. (Fig. 12.)

We then changed everything about. I went upstairs with a bottle of her hair, one pendulum, a male and a female sea urchin and considerable surprise. She went into the hall and tuned her pendulum to 29, the rate for her hair in the bottle I had taken with me. She got both answers right, but with rather less violence than I had experienced. Of course we did not stop at so few trials, but it is unnecessary to do hundreds of them at this stage.

53

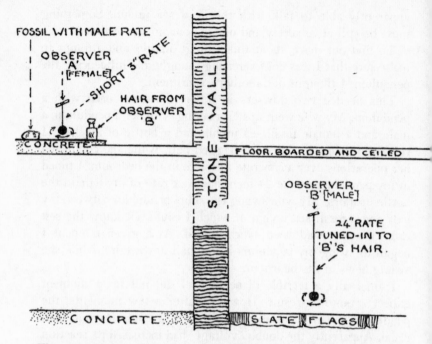

Fig. 12. Simple diagram to illustrate transmission between two pendulums in comparative isolation. Observer B's pendulum downstairs will take up with vigour, the oscillation, or gyration, obtained by observer A upstairs. The link appears to be the sample of B's hair

One point is at once clear. Two operators with two pendulums in tune add greatly to the ease of observation. Also it is evident that the necessary force to work the pendulum comes from the operator himself. We both felt tired after these experiments.

Of course curiosity would not let me rest. Was this reaction peculiar to sea urchins, or were other relics of dead organisms involved? I had a few fossil urchins, *Echinobrissus*, from the corallian beds at Upware, between Cambridge and Ely. These too reacted to a sex rate. But I could get none from a few specimens of what must have been young examples of a modern urchin, *Paracentrolus lividus*. This is a small relation of the edible sea urchin, well known to many, round our coasts, *Echinus esculenta*, whose eggs are very good with sherry. I thought the *Paracentrolus* specimens were probably too young to have developed sex.

I turned to fossil mollusca, the ordinary shells of the sea shore and also the pond and land shells. As a general rule I could get no sex reaction from the shell of any dead mollusc, fossil or recent. Large oriental cowrie shells had no more reaction than that of a dead snail on the garden path.

Since nothing could be learnt from shells apparently, I went through my drawers of relics, which I had collected in boyhood and boxes of things picked up in more recent times. I had skulls of various birds; hawks, crows, jays, pigeons, puffins, shearwaters and herons; wonderful examples of mechanical contrivance and things of beauty in themselves. Nearly all the owners of these skulls had been dead for at least forty years, and yet each one responded to a sex rate.

Then there were bones of mammals; stoats, weasles, moles, the skull of an arctic fox picked up in Jan Mayen in 1921, and the complete skeleton of a very old badger, which my wife had found lying in a lane in 1959 and I had buried until the bones were clear of flesh. I had had flu when she returned with this prize. The business of skinning it made me giddy, and, having no alum to preserve the skin, it had to be rubbed with wood ash. But I had the body buried before I returned to bed. I say this to show that there could be no doubt that the badger was really dead. The bones were not dug up again for over a year.

TABLE OF VARIOUS BONES TESTED NOVEMBER 1963

Species	Specimen	Pendulum rate	Remarks
Arctic fox	Skull	Female	Young. Found dead in Jan Mayen 1921
Badger	Skull	Male	Very old. Teeth worn right down. 1959
Badger	Pelvic girdle	No reaction	,, ,,
Badger	Other bones	,, ,,	,, ,,
Stoat	Skull	Female	Found dead 1919
Weasle	,,	Male	,, ,,
Mole	,,	Female	,, ,,

Now all the skulls responded to either the male, or the female rate for the pendulum. Although, however, I had the complete skeleton of the badger, only the skull had any sex rate at all and this was male. There was not even any response to the sex rate from the pelvic girdle where, if anywhere, such a response might have been expected. It appears that with mammals this sex rate is confined to the skull alone. (Fig. 13.)

I have quite a collection of other mammalian bones. For instance I have a series of metacarpal and metatarsal bones of sheep, which I have picked up on various excavations. They range in time from the Bronze Age, about 1500 B.C. right through the Iron Age, Roman, Saxon, Viking and Medieval times to the recent bones of soay and black-faced sheep. I collected them because I wanted to find out why and when the legs of sheep changed from thin deer-like types to the relative thick legs of today. No interest could be raised among the experts on ancient sheep; but, as far as my evidence goes, the change appears to have taken place in Tudor times, or even later. These bones give no sex reaction on the pendulum; neither do those of horse, red-deer, ox and so on. Lower jaws of various animals do not react. In fact the skull alone appears to do so.

It is the same story in the case of birds. I make a point of picking up bird bones in order to be able to identify specimens from ancient sites by comparing the bones with modern ones. Only the skulls give the sex rate:

TESTED NOVEMBER 1963

Species	Pendulum rate	Remarks		
Kestrel	Female	Found dead		1919
Kestrel	Male	,,	,,	1920
Jay	Male	,,	,,	1920
Crow	Female	,,	,,	1919
Pigeon	Female	,,	,,	1919
Puffin	Male	,,	,,	1919
Manx-shearwater	Female	,,	,,	1919
Heron	Female	,,	,,	1943

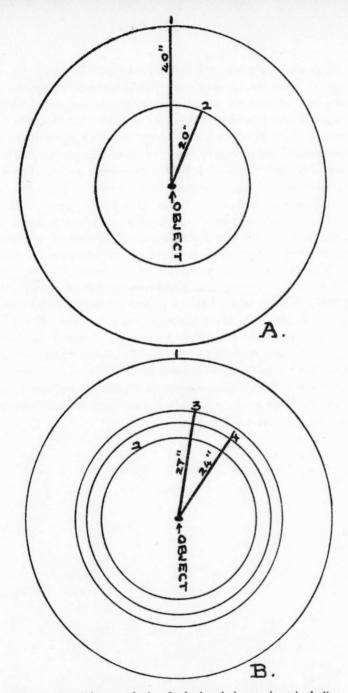

Fig. 13. Pendulum analysis of a badger's bones (not including minerals). A. Pelvic girdle. B. Skull. 1. Death rate. 2. Life rate. 3. Thought rate. 4. Male sex rate. 3 and 4 are only found in the skull. (The circles represent the base areas of each double cone)

Of course this is only a sample. To do the thing properly one ought to make hundreds of tests; but this requires a laboratory and a team of workers. I have to carry out this inquiry as simply as possible and it is only largely due to youthful enthusiasm that I have so many bones available to test. I don't suppose there are many houses in the country where one could lay one's hands on a dozen different types of skull at a moment's notice. However one does find, if one is prepared to observe such things, that everything one does, even if it is only picking up a fossil, or the skull of a bird, has its importance sometime in later life. There is no reason why I should have kept these small relics, but they fit into the picture now. Many people may never notice this kind of thing. Once you do begin to observe it, the effect is very striking. I do not think that I have ever done a small piece of research work which has not provided a bit to fit into some jig-saw puzzle later. Many of the objects I have been examining now were collected over forty years ago. Some of the fossils were even found more than fifty. Nearly all the owners of these shells and bones have been dead for forty years and some for more than a 100 million, and yet they give this sex rate on the pendulum. This is surely one of the most remarkable things that could be discovered.

Chapter Five

IT was very puzzling to find that this sex rate continued for such a stupendous length of time. To all seeming its persistence was endless. But it was almost as puzzling to find that only certain fossils and only skull bones of some types of vertebrate possessed a sex rate. I spent considerable time and thought over it and produced a working theory.

The sea urchin is entirely enclosed in its test, or shell. If any violent vibrations due to sex impulses occur in these animals, they take place inside this box. It seems clear that such vibrations must occur. In the case of molluscs, ordinary shells, the animal is not so completely enclosed. The valves, which snap to when the animal is alarmed, are kept partly open when the animal is alive and feeding. Anyone who has had the surprise of seeing a pecten, a scallop or queen, skipping over the surface of the sea to escape the attentions of a starfish, with its valves opening and shutting and its eyes gleaming round the edge of the shell, will know what I mean. In the case of the single valved molluscs, the winkles, whelks and so on, the land snails and the limpets, the animal walks about with most of its body outside the shell. It only retires inside, if it can do so at all, for security. Even the cowrie shell, which looks so like a complete protection, is enclosed by the animal when it is alive. There is no reason therefore why sex impulses from these animals should affect the shell. They take place unenclosed.

With birds and mammals the thinking apparatus is enclosed in a wonderfully intricate bony box, presumably the sex impulses take place in this also. Mammals do not think with their feet or stomachs. Impulses from these are sent up to the brain for

59

classification and necessary action. Of course there are openings in this brain case; but, like the shell of the sea urchin, it encloses the thinking part of the animal during its life. I happen to think that this brain is no more than a resistance and telephone exchange; but that does not concern the immediate problem. Nothing remains of the soft parts of any of these creatures for any length of time after death. But with many the brain case, resistance-box or shell of the sea urchin survives for a long period.

Thinking that the enclosure of the centre of impulses might be the clue, I looked round for other species to examine. Fishes have a brain case. I boiled the flesh off the skulls of several whitings, which the cat had had for breakfast—I am told that at Beer, the next village over the hill from Branscombe, no cat will eat any fish but whiting. All these fish skulls reacted to either the male or the female rate. Crab shells do so also. The animals live entirely inside.

What else has its life centre enclosed in this manner? For a long time I could think of nothing suitable and then I remembered that many insects, particularly beetles, have their body completely armoured with chitin.

At school, from about 1916–18 I had been very interested in beetles and had collected them. A few small cabinets were still in existence, buried in the junk in the tool shed. I dug them out.

In spite of a protection by napthalene, the little plague of zoological collections, the museum beetle, had been at work and many specimens were only represented by heaps of dust. However, enough remained for my purpose.

The large water-beetle, *Dytiscus marginalis*, is very well protected all over with chitinous armour. It is also incidentally noted for its power of flying long distances to small ponds (Fig. 8). It did not take many moments to see that I had examples of both male and female beetles, who can be at once recognized by differences on their fore-feet. The pendulum diagnosed the sex rate correctly. It was the same with another common beetle, *Timarcha tenebricosa*, which is popularly known as the 'bloody nose'. *Chrysomela banksi* did the same and so did all beetles which I tried. Beetles then retain this sex rate for at least forty-five years after death.

60

We have already observed that we are able to impress part of our electro-magnetic field on detached portions of our anatomy, such as a lock of hair. We have also seen that we can do the same with things that we make out of inanimate material. The carvings cut from gypsum showed this. How much we impress we do not know at present; but we do know that we impress the rate for sex, which is the only one of its kind that we have as yet discovered. It is reasonable to suppose that the same kind of thing happened with these sea urchins, skulls and insects. A part of their fields became detached and remained with them after their owners had long been dead. So long had some of them been dead that the persistence of the sex rate appears to show that this part of the electro-magnetic field is outside our earthly time. One might say that it was in a fourth dimension. It never was visible, audible, touchable and so on to any of our five bodily senses. Why then should these five senses be able to inform the brain as to whether the field as a whole persists indefinitely or not? Obviously these senses cannot do so and any argument using their evidence as to the persistence of life after bodily death is without value. It does not seem that the unaided brain of the most brilliant philosopher is competent to form an opinion. He has not got the right equipment to do so. But the pendulum is in touch apparently with something, which has the right equipment and can signal that parts of the fields of sea urchins persist for 100 million years. It can signal the answers to many other questions as well.

Slowly, like somebody trying to learn the Morse Code for the first time, we can learn from it the composition of chemical compounds. It can tell us the shape of the electro-magnetic fields surrounding a variety of substances. It can tell also where such substances lie hidden beneath a blanket of soil, or on the other side of a thick stone wall. By using the shape of the surrounding fields as a scale, we can estimate how deep hidden substances are beneath the soil. The knowledge possessed by this something is evidently more extensive than anything which reaches the brain during its normal functioning. If we add to this the activities of various para-normal faculties, foresight, telepathy, psychometry and so on, it is clear that the activities of this something are not confined to our earthly time scale and neither are they bounded by our scale of earthly measurement.

We are confronted obviously with a subject, which has not been included in the information we have been taught since childhood and to understand anything about it we have to begin from the beginning. Now we have all heard this before. This is something one remembers from the Christian Gospels. 'Unless you become again as little children ye cannot enter the kingdom of heaven.' Well that may be so indeed. Unless you can appreciate that there is part of your make-up which lasts indefinitely and knows much more than your brain, you are stuck in the world of materialism and atom bombs. But if you can appreciate that this something exists, a completely new view of life opens up. We can regard our body as a caterpillar and expect to go on through a chrysalis state to that of an imago, or complete entity. For the whole is the sum of its parts. If part of the whole persists for 100 million years, the whole must do so too. We must try to find what else can be transferred to the electro-magnetic field in order to see what might survive indefinitely.

The problem was to decide what else might be transferred to these other fields and then how to obtain its rate. Our given facts were that sex seems to be impressed by human fields on those of objects which it makes or uses, on carvings, pictures and so on. We found that the sex rate so impressed apparently remained long after the originator was dead. In some cases animals obviously impressed their sex rate so strongly that it remains to this day, after so long a time that we are incapable of visualizing it. A hundred million years, what does that mean to a human who may live for eighty?

Bearing in mind the claims of people who go in for psychometry that they can extract memory pictures from inanimate objects, it seemed hopeful to attempt to find a pendulum rate for memory. But, although it was not particularly difficult to find a rate of 27 inches which apparently corresponded to memory, it is not so easy to distinguish memory from thought. In practice almost all thought is more or less dependent on the memory of something or other. My wife and I tried the 27 inch length rate over one another. If one of us vividly recalled a picture of some incident or place, the pendulum held by the other gyrated as it would do for the sex rate. If then, by an effort of will, the victim managed to switch his or her attention on to a coal scuttle, or some other triviality, the pendulum instantly went into an oscillation. But if the victim tried to think of something else, such as how to set a mouse-trap in the shed, then memory was once more involved and the gyration took place. It did not seem that one could separate thought from memory very easily. And it also showed how I was right to be cautious about reading other people's work on this subject. Thought does appear to be able to affect the pendulum. However, there seems to be a distinction between thought and memory if it could be employed.

Perhaps this distinction is not a very important matter and for the present in any case we will regard thought and memory as being synonymous. We will use the 27 inch rate as thought rate and see what happens.

First it was necessary to see whether objects already impressed with the human sex rate also contained its thought rate in their field of force. Once again we tested an uncut lump of alabaster. It had no thought rate. However, a carved specimen registered this 27 inch rate strongly. (See Fig. 9.)

The next step was to see what happened with the skulls of birds, mammals and fishes. All skulls had responded to the sex rate and no other bones had done so. Exactly the same result was obtained for the thought rate.

We turned back to the fossils whose antiquity is so very great. In any case one does not believe that the estimates made by the geologists are right within tens of millions of years. All we can say that these things are of such enormous antiquity that the mind of man cannot appreciate it. It is outside his limited time scale. The world in which these fossils lived is so unlike the world of today that these animals might have been produced on Mars or Venus. The Downs, in whose chalk the fossils of the shepherd's heart can be found, were once the abyssmal depths of an unknown ocean. Yet the fossils of animals, which once lived in these seas an unappreciable time ago, still respond to the sex rate. This seems quite outrageously absurd, or are we all crazy?

Nevertheless, being obstinately devoted to inquiry into impossible questions, I took my fourteen specimens of shepherd's heart fossil sea urchins and tested them for our 27 inch thought rate with the pendulum. Thirteen responded to this rate. All had previously answered to the sex rate as being either male, female, or both. One had not given any rate for sex and now it gave no rate for thought. It was smaller than any of the others and perhaps too young to have any reactions when it died. One might think perhaps that the oncoming of the sex urge made the animals think for the first time. Of course we do not know: nobody knows. Can sea urchins think at all? I fancy that they must be able to think a little bit. How otherwise could they know how to use their tube feet to move themselves from place to place beneath the ocean?

I turned again to the fossil molluscs. No mollusc, fossil or recent, that I had tested so far had given any response to the sex rate. I thought that I had found the reason as I described before. The animals usually lived with their shells open or with their bodies outside the shells. Their thinking apparatus was not completely enclosed in the shell in the same manner as those of a sea urchin, or even a crab. Those of a mammal, or insect were also enclosed.

There was a number of fossil shells in the house. Some bivalves, as they are called, with double shells, had died with the valves open, while others were tightly closed. The answers to the pendulum were not the same as for the sex rate. Six specimens of the chalk fossil, *Terebratula carnea*, were tested. All were tightly closed. The four large specimens registered a 27 inch thought rate, but no sex rate. Two smaller specimens gave no response at all. (Fig. 14.)

Of half a dozen examples of *Spondylus spinosa*, another chalk fossil, only one was closed. Only this specimen gave any response and that was only to the thought rate.

There were a dozen examples of *Rynchonella octoplicata*, all were tightly closed. These gave no response to either rate. They may have all been juveniles, for much larger specimens are found. I do not know. Anyway they were dumb.

This may not be a very large number of specimens on which

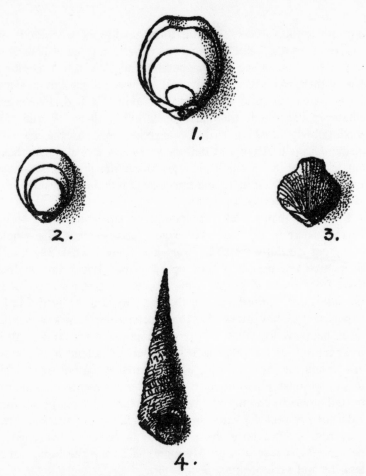

Fig. 14. Four Cretaceous fossils. 1 and 2. Terebratula carnea (1. Adult 2. Young). 3. Rynchonella octoplicata (young). 4. Turritella granulata. There is no pendulum reaction for sex from any of these fossils. Number 1, however, alone reacts to the 27-inch rate for 'thought'. Both 1 and 3 retain traces of their original colours

to base conclusions, but one has seen theories built up on much slighter evidence and I will hazard a guess. The animals all lived with their shells partly open and no sex vibrations were enclosed. However, something happened in the deep cretaceous seas, which made the older specimens scent danger. Perhaps the water became too hot, or too cold. An urgent impulse was sent out to the valves: 'Shut the doors quickly, boys. Something has gone wrong.' The younger specimens may have been too young to grasp what was happening and although discomfort caused them to close their valves, there was not enough urgency in the order for it to register in the animal's field. However, whatever happened, the emergency killed them all and the shells slowly filled up with Globigerina ooze, as the animals inside decayed. After 100 million years, we can now cut them out of the face of a chalk pit high above the present sea-level and enclosed within them find traces of such thought, or memory, as they once exercised.

I suppose that a really competent investigator would know exactly what to do next. He would have planned the whole thing out carefully from the start and known what was likely to happen and how to follow up each clue. But I am not like that; I do what I do in the same manner as that great scientist the late Lord Rutherford said that he played golf, by the light of nature. I do not know what to expect and I can only cope with what happens by what I hope is common sense and a little imagination. A roughly-made little ball on a length of cotton has jerked me into a world, which in theory cannot exist. Yet it surely must exist because all the experiments can be repeated again and again by anyone who can work the pendulum. I do not say that the rates are constant for every person. They may not be. But once the pendulum is tuned in for a given person all the rest is easy. My wife and I have the same wavelengths and several other people too.

The quest is becoming so difficult that I think we must stand back from the picture and try to form some idea of what seems to be appearing on it. Are we not really looking at some kind of extra dimension in which time and distance, as we know them in our daily lives, do not exist, and in which there are other ways of obtaining knowledge and establishing communication than anything we have heard of? Bits of us can apparently split off and be joined to something else. In fact they are doing it all the time. And the part of us from which they split is a part we never have any direct dealings with and it can it seems last for 100 million years.

Perhaps a very imperfect comparison may be of some help. Take somebody playing a beautiful air on a grand piano. You can see his hands, fingers and even his body working, and note the concentrated expression on his face. You can open the lid and watch the little hammers striking the taut wires. If you have the outlook of an archaeologist, you will note that the pianist is really playing an elaborated form of harp and recall the typology of the various more primitive instruments, which were the ancestors of that harp. You can observe the craftsmanship of the case, the tension of the wires and the padding of the hammers. If you were a doctor, you would note the general health of the pianist and remember how his bones, muscles and general physiology contributed to his playing. You could recall the laws of harmony, which tell you which series of notes sound well together. And finally you could take both man and instrument to pieces down to the most minute detail and speculate on the protons and neutrons, which went to compose the whole. After all this you would not be one iota nearer to knowing why the air the musician played brought a lump in your throat and tears to your eyes. The feelings, which caused these things to happen, belong to another dimension. They can never be measured according to the rules of any known science.

I am not much affected by this kind of thing myself, but I must admit that the great war-pipes always make me want to howl like a child. All the sorrow and pride of the ages seems to hit one with the first notes. It is not just regret for the kilted men one has known and lost. It is something far deeper and absolutely uncivilized as we know the world today.

I was once standing, at the South Uist Games, beside a delightful old English general, who was being looked after by a very wise and beautiful spaniel. The pipe band marched on to the field beside us. The old man turned to me and said, 'All the panoply of war. I think I understand these barbarians a little. I had some in my division.' But at that moment I was completely barbarian myself. My mother's people were calling me across the vanished years.

If there is a collective unconscious, as Jung believed, there are several sounds which can link me to it: the skirl of the pipes;

the whistle of the curlews; the screaming of the gulls and the roar of the sea. This last sound is surely that same 'Aum', which the Buddhists tell us is the voice of God. But it is only these very simple sounds which can do it. The almost unearthly beauty of the choristers' voices in King's College Chapel cannot do it; neither can the most appealing love songs ever written, however charming the voice of the singer. It is not the pipe tune. The thing hits you, like the blast of a bomb, at the very first fierce hum and buzz. I cannot explain why it should be so. It is not memory as memory is understood. In a moment of time, a few seconds, you appear to be linked with all the wild old warriors of the Celtic world. 'Here we are,' they seem to cry to their degenerate descendant, perhaps not so degenerate as all that; although I never saw my men used in battle. 'Here we are. Cuchulainn and Goll MacMorna, Sommerled and your own forefather, Alexander of Keppoch, killed by the English at Culloden, when "his children" deserted him.' But you do not think like that. Whatever this thing is it is instantaneous.

There are many other sounds, which one loves dearly. I am very fond of the merciless croaking of the ravens, who often answer me when I call. There is the glorious chatter of the wild geese far up in the sky, free and happy they shout to one another: 'This is a long way from Iceland, chums, but we'll soon be there now.' Once, sitting at my Cambridge desk, writing to a friend at Margam in Glamorgan, I heard the clamour of wild geese and ran out to look. About 100 white-fronts passed over my head heading south-westerly. I added to my letter: 'A hundred white-fronts just passed me heading your way.' By return of post a letter came back. 'They arrived here next evening.' Then there is the demon laughter of the great northern diver, ringing out over the still loch on a calm afternoon. That is a sound to remember. Of course it is, and memory is the key word. But there is no time for memory when the pipes suddenly start up. This is something different and outside the ordinary run of thinking. Some completely barbaric genius long ago discovered a sound, which could link the dead with the living. There it is and one cannot explain it. Sometimes a fiddle can have much the same effect, but it is not so devastating, not so completely and utterly devastating as the pipes.

Sound is a force in its own right, and some believe that it is a 'killer'. Whether this is so or not, it is clearly of great importance to find, with the help of some passing aeroplanes and the drumming of a great spotted woodpecker, that it has the same rate of 30 inches as hydrogen. Hydrogen is widely believed to be the basic element of the universe. In fact our pendulum's table of rates gives us four which seem to be of basic importance. There is 10 inches for light; 20 for all organic material, alive or dead; 30 for sound and 40 for sleep and death. This is so remarkable that we must surely conclude that this scale was evolved by something outside our earthly three dimensions.

Chapter Six

WITH the best will in the world, one cannot write a book like this as a completely consecutive story. Diversions from the main investigation are bound to occur especially when it is not very clear what the main line ought to be. People write to me and say, 'Can dowsers locate water from a map?' Or questions of this kind. But as far as possible I will try to keep the story consecutive; although this takes it out of its true chronological sequence. Not long ago, my publisher, Colin Franklin, set me off on a problem, which seems to be in the correct line. Put shortly, he wanted to know whether the reproductions of pictures still retained the sex rate of the painters of the originals. Now this is surely an important question and goes quite a long way to further the investigation. To enlarge it somewhat, one might ask whether a book carries with it part of the original field of force of the author. If it should do so, then a book might be compared with the laying on of hands in consecrating a priest. People have told me that there is a gap of 200 years in this ceremony and that power is no longer handed on in direct succession. I do not know about this; but the possibility that part of the author's psyche-field might go with each copy of a book which he had written struck me as being very interesting. I did not believe it for a moment.

Now unless you are prepared to wander round public art galleries with a folio of reproductions and a pendulum, it is not so very easy to find the answer to Colin Franklin's question. I thought about it for some time before I hit on a possible way of testing it. I draw the illustrations, of doubtful value, which accompany my books. I asked him to send me back the original drawings from one of them. I supposed that they were filed somewhere and not destroyed when the blocks were made.

My idea was to test first an original drawing for the sex and thought rates and then to test the reproduction made from that drawing in a completely new and unopened copy of the book itself. Of course many people handled the drawings in the course of making the blocks from them and some slight handling may have occurred in the printing and binding of the book. That we had to risk, but the risk did not appear to be great.

In due course a folder of drawings arrived and I took them to the slate floor in the hall, where there should not be much interruption from anything but the slate. In a state of considerable interest, I put the first drawing on the floor and tested it for the rate for male sex of 24 inches and then for thought at 27 inches. It responded strongly to both. Then I opened the new copy of the book at the figure made from the drawing and tested that. There was no reaction of any sort to either rate. The figure appeared to be dead. My wife and I went solemnly through the drawings and the prints made from them. All the drawings responded to the sex and thought rates. Nothing at all happened with the prints. There was no reaction for either rate from the book itself. There was not the slightest indication that any fragment of the author's personality passed to the book, except that the printed word might mean something to the person who read it. There was no direct contact at all. The book was not a link in any parapsychological sense between the author and the reader. There was nothing passing between an artist who painted a picture and the reproduction of that picture. The quality of the reproduction, however good it might be, is something entirely mechanical and lacking in the life force which has been impressed by the artist on the original.

We have already seen the same kind of thing suggested by thinking about photographs. The photograph appears dead, so is the reproduction by mechanical means of an original picture. A hand-made copy would of course react to the sex rate of the person who made the copy.

This experiment was rather a relief to me. I had not been able to see how anything could really pass from original to reproduction. Whereas everything we had investigated before followed a logical course, however strange that course might appear to be, this transference of something to a reproduction seemed completely illogical. Yes, I was relieved. Crazy though we might seem to be; yet we were not so daft as all that. We had managed to put a brake on.

Still, it could not be left at that. As far as the pendulum went, nothing of any sort passed from an author directly into the field of a book he wrote. His ideas were mechanically broken down into a code, which was mechanically transferred to paper. From that paper the mind of somebody else decoded the words once again and more or less understood what the author wanted to say. Our sixth sense communication is something quite different from this and arrives as fully formed ideas without words, or as pictures.

I found all this interesting, for I had recently been sent a letter from a stranger. This letter informed me that its author had read two of my books. From them he could tell by radiesthesia that I was suffering from various ailments and would shortly be afflicted with more and worse ones. Well that is all very alarming; one reaches for the gin bottle at once! But even if my unknown friend had got his guesses right, he could not have found the answers in that manner, for, as we have seen nothing passes from the author's psyche-field into the field of the printed book.

I tested a number of new books. They were all blank. Then I tried an almost new book, which, as far as I knew, had only been read by one man. This gave a strong reaction on the thought rate and one on the male rate. It also rather unexpectedly reacted to the female rate. Then I remembered that the book had been given to me by a woman friend. She had probably looked at it first. Library books all reacted to the thought rate and most of them to both male and female. However, one only gave a female reaction, although several people had taken it out from the library. It did not look the kind of book that many men would read.

This of course is in reality what people call psychometry, but we are only doing it in a halting and uncertain manner. While we can only say that the pendulum tells us first that a book starts as a blank and then that it has been studied by a man and a woman and they have thought about it; the psychometrist senses a tiny film-like series of pictures related in some way to the users of the book. We are, I think, in a position to state that psychometry is a perfectly genuine faculty and one which should be given a lot of study. But there is a great and obvious snag to it. The field of the inanimate object handled by the psychometrist has almost always been handled also by more than one person. Each of these persons has probably left some detached part of his own field in that of the object, and there is no means of telling to what extent these various intrusions have been mixed together. It is even more complicated than the study of dreams, I know something about this. I used a very good sensitive for a large number of experiments in the early 30's. Although some of my deductions were then faulty, the information obtained was fact and this I can now look at again in the light of what dowsing has to say. If we could think out a few more rates for the pendulum, we might discover much more. One might be able to tabulate the general appearance of a reader of a book for instance, in the same general way that police reconstruct the appearance of a wanted criminal. In fact the pendulum might be very helpful to the police. Or we could build up the face and character of an unknown correspondent. To return to my radiesthesia friend for a moment. No doubt he had found all these distressing diseases with his machine. But since he had no link with me, they undoubtedly came from someone who had borrowed the books from a library, probably more than one person. It was interesting to see that he did not mention the one complaint which has afflicted me since 1920, rheumatism.

Of course letters come into the same picture. You can take a letter from an unknown person and with the short pendulum apparently see whether the writer has an affinity with you or not. I do not think that it is wise to put much store in this. One does not know how much the pendulum can be affected by the operator's thought. Quite a small phrase in the letter might give enough irritation to the reader to cause an adverse reaction on the pendulum. Words are terribly misleading, for they are coded thoughts. When decoded some words may be of quite a different value to what was meant by the writer. There is another possibility of error. With the short pendulum an affinity is shown between male and female and the reverse is indicated with two animals of the same sex. Therefore the pendulum tends to indicate affinity between man and woman and the reverse between man and man. However, the affinity is clearly strong enough at times to overcome this general tendency, even to the extent of great enthusiasm being shown by the pendulum when swung between two letters from people of the same sex. The short rate on the pendulum is evidently of more general significance than the long individual rates. The thought rate appears to be stronger than the sex rate.

All this is of much general interest; but I do not regard it as coming as yet into the world of science in the same way as I regard the more exact behaviour of the long pendulum.

Yet many dowsers work entirely with the short, unrated pendulum and correct its vagaries by mechanical means. I think that they are mistaken and are behaving like an anxious first mate trying to correct the balance of his vessel by shifting the cargo, when the dangerous rolling in a sea-way is in reality due to an error on the designer's part on the drawing-board. It is a rate on the long pendulum, which will tell us eventually whether the writer of a letter has blue eyes or brown or whether he would like to stick a knife under your ribs, or present you with a case of champagne. The pendulum is simply an indicator of what something outside our five senses is ready to tell us and the simpler that indicator is, the more likely it is that the information will come through as that something intended. Wise women, sensitives, or what you like, get this information direct without any intervention from an indicator. But our pendulum goes a long way towards showing that the information, which these sensitives give, is liable to be correct, even if it is also confused. Once it becomes clear that there is a something, a something which does not require a brain to act as a computor and which knows many things which the five senses cannot supply to the brain for its computing, we have taken a considerable step forward. In fact we have left the three-dimensional world of length, breadth and thickness and begun to explore a fourth dimension. This perhaps is the next stage of evolution, to become four dimensional. It may sound utter rubbish to people with ideas firmly rooted in the three, but we are beginning to find evidence for its existence. If one single event can be shown to have been correctly forecast before it took place in earthly time, you are in another dimension where cause may precede effect and this is impossible in three-dimensional science. But innumerable cases are known where this has happened and I have even done it myself as a small transistor radio beside my wife's bed bears witness, for it was bought with the profits. The future and the past can often be observed by people using the sixth sense and I very much doubt whether the most case-hardened materialist does not really know this in the secret parts of his make-up. He may flap and bluster and growl, if he is honest he must appreciate that no theoretical extension of the functions of the brain can explain all the curious facts with which we have been dealing. If all the soft parts of a sea urchin decayed 100 million years ago and the only life of that sea urchin was in those soft parts, how could we possibly detect its rates for sex and thought today? The only explanation must be that there was something about that sea urchin which was independent of those soft parts and that it still functions after that enormous lapse of time. The only explanation that I can see at present is that that something is mind, spirit if you like, and that that mind is only linked to the brain, or whatever you like to call it for a sea urchin, by the electro-magnetic field. (Fig. 15.) It is our mind, being independent of the three dimensions, which knows about matters which cannot be deduced from three-dimensional data. This mind, our real life, exists in four dimensions, and as such has no bounds in time or space. It is not easy when one has been brought up from childhood to think in terms of three dimensions to be suddenly expected to do so in four. But apparently all we have been discussing relates to the properties of the fourth. The signals without words, which go out over immense distances regardless of the laws of mechanical electro-magnetism; the foreknowledge

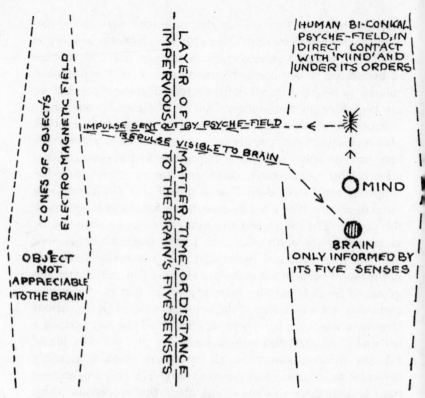

Fig. 15. Simple diagram attempting to explain the manner in which all extra sensory perception appears to work. This diagram is of course highly conjectual. There appears to be no direct contact between MIND and BRAIN

of the future; the ability to contact things out of reach of the senses; all the intangible phenomena connected with these fields of force; none of these really pertains to a three-dimensional world. They belong to a fourth in which life belongs to a mind with a different rate of vibration.

Throughout the ages, and in many lands, some men have always appreciated that there was something beyond the three-dimensional world, but the more you become attached to the three the harder it is to grasp the existence of the fourth. Even those hard-headed, rugged rascals, the Vikings, believed in a future life. The idea is at least 10,000 years old in this country and probably far older elsewhere. The skeleton of the Red Lady, a man, in Pavisland cave in Gower, was reddened with ochre to be properly dressed in war paint for the next world.

Now, this idea seems completely illogical for a hunting people. Many psychological theories have been put forward to account for it and not one appears to fit. A hunting people lives on what it kills. Once the animal is dead, it is eaten and that is the end of that. Men kill each other and they are dead and probably eaten too. There seems to be no reason why a hunter should surmise that he in particular should go to another world. Everything around him always dies and the most that is likely to remain is a small heap of greenish-white bones under a rock. I do not believe the theory that man was so sure of his importance that he could not believe in his dissolution and so created an imaginary conception of a Happy Hunting Ground beyond this Land of Woe. Most countrymen take the life cycle from birth to death very calmly. It is the natural way in which things are arranged. It goes on around them all the time and they accept it as a matter of course. There may be a next world, or there may not, they live in the present. But apparently all tribes even the Eskimo, who had no belief in gods till quite recently, believe in the spirits of the dead and think that they can get in touch with them.

The only reasonable explanation that I can find to account for this belief in a future life, is that when living in a less hustled and more uncomplicated state men did keep in closer touch with their real minds than they do today. From these minds they could appreciate something which we do not now grasp. In fact they knew that when they died, they were not extinguished. They became spirits. They did not know much about this spirit existence; but they knew that it was there.

From this point, the whole totem system evolved, for of course, if they continued to live as spirits, the animals did so too. The belief in spirits would be added to naturally when somebody saw a ghost. But it seems improbable that the seeing of a ghost gave rise to the belief in spirits. The ghost could not communicate with them. It never spoke. But something else

77

gave them visions of future events and showed them what they took to be another world.

One reason why I think the palaeolithic hunters of France and Spain obtained their religious ideas by some kind of contact with their fourth-dimensional minds, is that they were obviously much devoted to the working of sympathetic magic. Everyone now knows of their paintings of their animal neighbours deep inside caves. There has been such a spate of books stressing the artistic side of this painting that the magic purpose tends to be forgotten. But the purpose was to secure the food supply by magic means. That is why there are so many bison on the roof of the Altamira cave in Spain. The image of the bison was painted there apparently with a kind of crayon made from its own fat. This is the magic of the Ages and we have seen that there is a link between a detached portion of a person and his own psyche-field. It is a property now used by radiesthetists to effect healing at a distance. But this was not always so. Something from the body of an enemy, blood, hair, nail or spittle, gave the magician a link to him and he could in theory work evil to him through this link. It was not the picture so much that was important as the substance with which it was drawn. Like would call to like and in theory the palaeolithic hunter could call up a bison when one was needed. Other aspects of this early art suggest that fertility of man and beast was also desired and magic steps were taken at times to ensure it.

The strange thing about all this is that, if you really knew how to co-operate with the real mind, it seems highly probable that you could work the magic. I have told elsewhere how I found my mother, who used to suffer a great deal with rheumatism, apparently almost free from it. On being told that she had given a drop of blood to someone who worked 'The Box', I remarked that it was magic. She replied that she did not care what it was, but it had cured her rheumatism. 'The Box' is a modern version of a very ancient art. The pendulum tells us that my mother's drop of blood was, in this fourth-dimensional world, still in touch with her main electro-magnetic field. Orders given to the drop of blood, long separated from her and completely dead, were obeyed by her field and through it communi-

78

cated to her body, which obeyed them and threw out the uric acid. The bison hunter believed that he knew how to attract the bison. The process was repeated so often that we may think that he probably did know and the operation was a success. It seems improbable that so much trouble would be taken every time the hunter went out. The ritual was probably seasonal and was performed yearly as many times as there are bison on the roof of that cave.

Chapter Seven

NATURE apparently always consists of a balance of opposites. Where there is night there is also day: where there is evil there is also good. Positive and negative, male and female it is the same story. So it is not surprising to find in our study that it is not one-sided. Although you can tune in on what appears to be a repulsion rate to substances, there are other substances which act as a complete obstacle to this. I call them interrupters, but this is not the right term, for they are really conductors and counteract the repulsion effect which gives us our rates.

The first interrupter I found was lead. Lead has the same, or nearly the same rate as several metals; but while it is an interrupter, silver with the same rate of 22 inches is not. The effect of an interrupter is instant and quite dramatic. If you tune in to a gold object and, while the pendulum is gyrating, put a piece of lead beside the gold, the gyration changes in a moment to a back and forth swing. If you hold a piece of lead in your left hand while the pendulum, suspended from your right hand, is gyrating over the piece of gold, and then transfer the lead from the left hand to the right, the gyration stops at once and oscillation begins.

If I have reasoned correctly before, we find the rates of substances because they cause a block in a circulatory system of electric current, which includes your personal field and that of the earth. This may be wrong, but the current must flow between you and something of that sort. The pendulum oscillates because the pressure tries to get through and on that particular rate there is an obstruction, which forces it aside and round through a circle. It makes the water-diviner's rod turn over for the same reason. The rod is in unstable equilibrium with the current passing through its apex and the obstruction of the flow causes it to turn aside and rotate. The force is very great and breaks the rod if you try to hold it tight and prevent its rotation. This is not difficult to understand, perfectly reasonable and within the bounds of science. It is also magic, for divination is one of the magic arts. I think that all magic arts could be interpreted in terms of science, if it could be bothered to study them.

Now our lead somehow neutralizes the obstruction. In man-made electricity it is an insulator and prevents current leaking away from copper wires. Why it should do so, I do not know. Presumably it was found long ago that it did so and it may have been used without question ever since. It may be known why it works, but I do not know. An archaeologist cannot be expected to have a wide knowledge of physics. Yet an observed fact in physics is the same as an observed fact in our study. Lead is an insulator in both. In our study the very presence of a lump of lead, within the radius of its pendulum rate prevents current flowing from our electro-magnetic field into that of a piece of gold.

Thinking that since gold has a rate of 29 inches and a conic radius at the base of 29 inches, there might be a zone outside the 22 inch radius of lead in which the gold rate could still be found. I tried this. There is no such zone. The lead neutralizes the field of gold at its centre. There are not two double cones of force one inside the other, with a dead lead cone inside and a live gold cone outside. The effect of the lead is complete.

Now you can take the short pendulum and get a victim to lie on the floor. If you keep the pendulum oscillating across his backbone, at any point in the victim's back where there is damage and the current in the nervous system does not run freely, the pendulum will gyrate. I have done this with some people and apparently the pendulum tells the truth. Arthritis can be located easily. This is not imagination. The back can be examined by X-rays and the pendulum proved to be telling the truth. It has been done with one of my victims and arthritis revealed at each point where the pendulum indicated an obstruction. I am not setting up as a healer or anything of that sort. I am simply an inquisitive person trying to find out what is going on. As far as I can see the pendulum is an aid to diagnosis and since dowsing is related to such things as diagnosis with 'The Box', this apparatus is reliable.

Now you can find the arthritic joint, or whatever it is, easily with the pendulum; but, if when this is gyrating over that point, you place a piece of lead beside the injury, or against the hand holding the pendulum, the gyration stops at once and oscillation begins. The effect with a human being is exactly the same as with inanimate matter such as gold. This is surely not the same as enclosing a copper wire in a tube of lead. It is not simple insulation, which takes place, but something of a different order. The field of the lead blocks out the obstruction. It has the same effect if you use it with a letter, which registers opposition or hostility. This is no longer physics as it is now known. It is something more extensive connected with the whole study of life.

I am sure I do not know whether it would prevent the spread of arthritis if you wore a lead object about your person, but it does seem as if lead neutralizes the effect and permits current to flow freely.

Lead is an insulator to radio-active rays and is regarded as a dead metal. It appears to absorb these rays and it was interesting to see that when I was asked to test a sheet of lead, which had been bombarded for some time by them, it did not react to the 22 inch rate. There is something here of very great importance, which might have a radical effect on healing.

However, lead is not by any means the only interrupter. But of metals it appears to be the strongest. Aluminium is another; although it is weak compared with lead and has a different rate.

A friend complained to me that he was unable to find a gold watch when it was hidden from him. In theory the gold case should have reacted to the 29 inch rate. But it did not. This would have seemed insoluble if we had not already learnt of the existence of interrupters. But having got so far, it seemed clear that something was getting in the way. I tried other watches. It made no difference what the case was made of. None of them reacted to the appropriate wave-length. Since their works only appear to contain iron, brass and the bearings for their wheels, it seemed clear that the interrupter was in these bearings. I had always heard of the bearings being spoken of as rubies. One had seen lists of stolen articles: 'A gold watch jewelled in nine holes, and a gold Albert (meaning a watch chain)', and so on. What were the bearings made of? A search revealed that they were either made of indifferent rubies, or a hard form of garnet. Both were complicated compounds containing the metal calcium. I had some garnets, which came from a glen on the south side of the head of Loch Morar. These showed at once to the pendulum that they were interrupters. But they were relatively weak. Still interrupters they were and whether the bearings were of ruby or garnet, this was the reason why my friend could not find his hidden watch with the pendulum. We knew that to find a gold object, which had no interrupters was relatively easy, for my wife had once accidentally thrown away a ring of gold into a bed of nettles and brambles and we had found it in less than five minutes. There must be, however, some method of circumventing the interrupters, for I have been told of a gold watch being recovered from a dustbin with a pendulum. I do not suppose that the long rate was used. It may have been the short one and the watch have been located by the 'affinity' method.

We will leave the interrupters for a moment and go on to another facet of this study, which also happens to contain the same problem. My wife was entirely responsible for this and I doubt whether I should ever have thought of it. She remarked, when we were getting a meal, 'Why do you think that some trees are considered unlucky?' On my grunting that I had no idea, she continued: 'Do you think you could find out with the pendulum?' Her question opened an entirely new line of approach and I do not suppose that anyone has followed it. Whoever in these scientific days would ever believe for a moment that a tree could be unlucky? This was some superstitious nonsense, which could not possibly have any foundation in fact. Nevertheless the beliefs are most widespread. I have long grown up past the stage of scoffing at such things.

I started to recall what I could remember of folk-beliefs. Of course elder was most unlucky. You must never cut it down without asking its permission. You must never burn it, or somebody would die. An alternative version had it that you burnt the Devil and so presumably irritated him. So widespread are these superstitious beliefs that you might say that they are everywhere in the country. Elder was evidently believed to have an inveterate hostility to mankind.

Yet elder has its uses. Its flowers make a kind of bubbly wine sometimes likened to champagne. Its berries are mixed with various pies to add flavour. The yellow inlay in marquetry furniture is often elder. Incidentally elder when freshly cut stinks. Some say it smells of corpses.

Now rowan, mountain-ash, is just the opposite. From East Anglia to the Island of Skye, I have heard rowan spoken of with great respect. A sprig of it over the door will keep evil magic away. A friend, who runs a pack of beagles, told me that when some disease struck them, which the vet could not cure, she surrounded the kennels with pieces of rowan and they recovered at once. I do not know whether the wood is used for any particular purpose, but my aunt used to make a good jelly from the berries.

Here were two common trees credited with absolutely different properties. Could there be any possible reason for these beliefs?

I cut pieces from each tree and tested them with the long pendulum. Elder gave a male reaction and rowan a female one. The short pendulum indicated repulsion between elder and myself, while rowan showed attraction.

This started me off on a search for other samples. I cut a piece from Zeus's own tree, the oak; and others from holly, thorn and elm. Oak has, of course, been a most useful timber for thousands of years, but I was really thinking of the elm. Kipling was a good folk-lorist and not for nothing did he write:

'Ellum she hateth mankind and waiteth till every gust be laid
 To drop a limb on the head of him who any where trusts to
   her shade.'

But he had the sex wrong. The pendulum said that elm was
male.

Elm is not much used inland except for floor-boards and
coffins; although there is some elm furniture and I have an old
sideboard made of it. But from Kent to the Scilly Isles boats
are still planked with elm. It builds very sturdy boats for beach
work. Nevertheless elm is regarded with some suspicion.

Oak reacted to the female rate on the long pendulum and
showed attraction on the short. Thorn was the same, but the
reaction was slight. Holly was weakly male and hostile.

In all I tested fourteen trees. Six were male and indicated
repulsion. Eight were the opposite as the following table shows:

Tree	Pendulum Male	Reaction Female
Elder	x	–
Rowan	–	x
Oak	–	x
Ash	x	–
Elm	x	–
Thorn	–	x
Hazel	–	x
Holly	x	–
Fig	x	–
Pine	x	–
Willow	–	x
Apple	–	x
Ivy	–	x
Beech	–	x
Total: 14	6	8

Now from a botanical point of view this was all nonsense.
Many trees are hermaphrodite and bear both male and female
flowers. What sense could there be in what the pendulum
appeared to be telling us?

I took a branch of elder and pulled it to pieces. I had flowers,

85

fruit, bark, pith and wood. I tested these separately. Only the wood was male and hostile. I have yet to think of a reason why this should be so.

Remembering the belief that, although elder was hostile, rowan was protective, I tried another experiment. I put a sprig of elder opposite myself and swung the short pendulum between the two. The pendulum went into a circular swing, indicating, according to the ideas I have already described for inanimate objects, that there was an obstruction to the flow of current between my field and that of another which I have guessed as being the earth's field. Then I placed a sprig of rowan beside the piece of elder. Immediately the previous gyrations stopped and a back and forth movement began. Therefore the rowan masked the elder's obstructive power and restored a normal flow of current. The same thing happened when the long pendulum was used. The rowan obscured the elder's male sex rate and the pair together became female. So rowan in the vegetable world has the same property as lead in the mineral one. It is what I have been calling an interrupter.

Thinking that magnetism probably had some say in this curious phenomenon. I placed a horseshoe magnet opposite myself with its ends open and swung the short pendulum. The pendulum gyrated. When the ends were closed, the oscillation began. In a sense then the rowan sprig when applied to the elder could be compared with a soft iron bar placed across the ends of a horseshoe magnet. If this comparison is permissible it looks as if these interrupters somehow close the electro-magnetic fields around objects in the same way that the soft iron bar joins the ends of the horseshoe magnet and forms a closed circuit.

In any case we seem to see that if elder can exert any deleterious influence from its field, rowan can stop this. But it can only do so within the 29 inch radius of its field. Within this radius its feminity is too strong for the elder. Something of this situation appears to have been appreciated by less sophisticated persons than those of the present day. Somehow they learnt that rowan could close the gaps in their protection from hostile influences. How it could possibly do so we have yet to find out.

It does not seem in the least credible, but very little in this study did when we began it.

The comparison with terrestial magnetism as it is understood is probably far too easy. In the first case we have the perfectly simple matter of closing a circuit in one plane. The horseshoe magnet is only a bar magnet bent round in a half circle and all that the soft iron rod does is to join one pole to another. A piece of soft iron joining the two ends of a straight magnet would have the same effect. But in the case of the fields we are exploring a small object placed beside another appears to swamp a whole biconical field with its own. The field of a human-made magnet is imperceptible to the five senses. That of an object is so also. Neither magnetism nor electricity are directly perceptible to the five senses; although their shocks to the body can be appreciated. The biconical fields surrounding the objects we are studying can only be appreciated by indicators of some kind. The electro-magnetic fields of the inanimate objects may come into the normal curriculum of physics. The fields of human beings and animate objects are not so easy to study. We are probably trying to investigate a facet of life itself and the means available are quite inadequate. Electricity and magnetism no doubt come into it, but are only a small part of the whole. The life itself appears to be four dimensional. Therefore we have no idea how powerful these biconical fields may be, nor what effect they may have on the human body. Without knowing this, it is impossible to say that elder is not hostile to humanity nor that rowan is friendly.

If we look at our table again, which is in itself very incomplete, we see two trees whose fruits were to the ancient Celtic world symbols of immortality. One is hazel and the other apple. Most people must have heard of the Apple of Life, which the Goddess Brigid held in her hand and know of the apples in the Garden of the Hesperides. Hazel nuts were similarly regarded as friendly to mankind. Both of them, like rowan, have a female rate and are interrupters. They muzzle hostility, or let current flow between the human field and whatever the main field may be. If the main field is in reality the source of life and the provider of the energy which keeps things alive, then the value of the interrupters becomes understandable. Given that mankind was once much more sensitive to such things than it is today, its reaction can have been much more like that of our cat sensing another at a distance. Man may have felt with his sixth sense which things were friendly to him and which were harmful. For instance how do birds know which berries are good to eat and which are poisonous. Domestic animals have lost this faculty. They eat, at least cows do, yew clippings and die from it. But surely they never did this in a wild state. The great black aurochs, the ancestor of domestic cattle, which was so huge that classical writers compared it with an elephant, was a woodland beast. There must have been plenty of yew trees in the primeval forest which it could have eaten and died from the effects. Are we to suppose that a percentage always died from eating this tree, or that the aurochs knew that it was a poisonous plant and left it alone? Or are we to surmise that man learnt by trial and error that he must not eat deadly nightshade, henbane, and the other poisonous plants? Was the early road of mankind strewn with corpses of people who had tried eating various fruits out of altruistic regard for their fellows? Did men come up to one of their companions writhing in agony and say, 'What did you eat, old chap, so that we will know it another time?' This seems most improbable. They knew by the sixth sense and traces of their knowledge remain to this day. Just as something buzzed near my head and told me the future winner of the Grand National, so something buzzed for prehistoric man and warned him not to eat *Amanita phalloides*, that most deadly of poisonous fungi. Really good water-diviners, as I have said before, can tell without a rod where water lies, by the tingling in the nerve-ends of their fingers. I have little doubt that this faculty was much more developed in primitive men. Has anyone ever heard of a wild animal eating anything poisonous before man started scattering poisons broadcast? But primitive man thought about what the sixth sense told him. When he was warned that something could kill him, he thought: 'Then I will not eat it myself, but I will put it on something and poke it into that bear, which is always trying to come into our cave.' Something outside themselves told them more than they could learn by direct observation. This something has to a large extent been cut off from us, but it is still available, even if at the moment we can only talk to it with a pendulum. The cat could not observe the other cat hunting on the hill 450 yards away, but it could sense it. The Manx shearwater could not know where its chick was, but it was led unerringly back to it over thousands of miles of sea. People cannot know by any of the ordinary senses what will happen in a month's time, yet some do know. It is all part of one unexplored subject, which could be investigated on an infinitely wider scale than I can even think about, much less hope to do.

Chapter Eight

IT must occur to some readers that everything I have written may be entirely imaginary. Being a born doubter myself, I completely understand such a view. But it is impossible for it to be imaginary. If you can use the pendulum to work out within an inch or two exactly where something lies hidden beneath undisturbed turf, and do this in front of witnesses, and then go to the spot which the pendulum has indicated and take off the turf, dig up the soil beneath and find the object. If you can do this same operation again and again and almost always succeed, this cannot be imagination, delusion, or any of these things. It is scientific experiment however crude it may be. There are of course numerous points which we do not understand. The interrupters may interrupt and on occasion prevent your finding something. There are many rates, which are much the same and so instead of finding some silver object answering to the silver rate, you may find some compound of sodium and so on. But the thing works and the proof of any pudding lies not in its appearance but the taste of it. Therefore, however strange may be the information that the pendulum gives, we may be confident that it is not imagination, which is playing tricks with us. In this book it has already told us so many almost incredible things that one begins to feel quite nervous of it.

For one thing it is so amazingly simple. In analysis of a compound, for example, if you have the rates worked out, you can get a very good idea what it is in a few minutes. It may be a little difficult to tell sodium from calcium. But one is an interrupter, while the other is not. You can tell at once whether it has sulphur or carbon in it. It is not my job to work out all these

90

rates. I am trying, as I said before, to get at the main points in all this. But I am confronted with a very strange world, far stranger I feel than anything produced by physics, botany or biology. These cones of force, there must be millions of them in any backyard, which can be contacted instantly by a ray projected from our own psyche-field, are much more difficult to comprehend than molecules, atoms and electrons, for we were more or less brought up to take these for granted, even if they are just as impossible to sense. These theories are at first inferred and then comes the proof of the pudding. Do they react as they ought to do? So far, in practice, they have stood up to the test, or people would not be so worried about atom bombs. But they may not do so for more than a generation. Our cones are not so vague. Anyone who can work the pendulum can find them in his own house. Of course he may have to do it in a concrete floored kitchen, or in the lavatory, because of the peculiar behaviour of elm floor-boards.

So we live in a world and walk about in it, where everything could look to a four-dimensional eye like a tightly packed forest. We can stretch out our arm with a finger pointing and select one of these cones at a considerable distance; judging by the Manx shearwater at thousands of miles. The vixen, in theory, just sends out her ray and the dog-foxes gallop for miles to it. If the ray were visible, it would be easier to understand it. But perhaps we have forgotten how someone turned a radar beam up into the sky from a Canadian airfield when geese were migrating and they came to earth in hundreds utterly confused. The radar beam is invisible and so are ours. So there is nothing really difficult to understand about all this. It is just strange. It would be far less strange to people of the East, where 'holy men' have been thinking about such things for thousands of years, but without the background of modern science.

The men of the East believe that, after years of contemplation, they can bring their own personal selves into a higher level of existence. They believe they can look out of a window and see a cow walk through a wall. They also believe that they can dissolve their bodies into atoms, fly instantaneously through the air, and reconstitute the body in some distant place. Well, to

91

us this sounds the most utter piffle. We are northerners, who won what position we may still hold in the world by what we may call 'guts and ginger'. Few of us have ever bothered even to look at the writings of the East. Writing as a northerner, with the bones of many relatives lying under foreign soils, not only in the south, but in the far north, I feel slightly antagonistic to these eastern ideas. Still I keep an open mind all the time. These easterners have thought a lot about it and they may have got some of the answers right. Our western outlook is obviously too materialistic today. This view, based on far too little information, obviously needs breaking down. It is based ultimately on five senses and there are clearly at least six. It is confined to three dimensions and there must be at least four. This is the predicament in which one is landed if one thinks about this kind of thing at all.

As far as I know, there has been no study of dowsing in the eastern world and precious little in our own part of the globe. There is no mention of it in the classics that I know of. One would have thought that there might have been eminent Arab diviners. The Moslem peoples were far advanced beyond what they called the 'Franks', for several centuries. In mathematics they were very skilled and the study of algebra is theirs. I cannot have an encyclopaedic knowledge, but, as far as I know, in countries where water was scarce, they did not employ dowsers to find it. They cannot have known how to do so, for their outlook was apparently flexible.

Dowsing then, and you must not trust my knowledge in this matter, seems to be something evolved in the West. For some obscure reason, when science began to grow, dowsing was ruled out of the curriculum. Alchemy grew into chemistry, but divination grew into nothing. In the early days of science, many must have known that water could be divined. But apparently it was either anathema to Holy Church, which could not perhaps do it itself, despite the story of Moses, or else other matters seemed more interesting and it was overlooked. But one would have thought that the alchemists would have jumped at it. Perhaps they did, but not knowing about interrupters and that the female rate is the same as for gold, they were discouraged. In any case dowsing did not attract general interest. It is hinted at in Leland's *Aradia*, a gospel of the Italian witches, where it says that one of the benefits of the worship of Diana would be the power to locate hidden treasure and money concealed by priests. People from the eighteenth century onwards seem to have tried to locate gold by some form of dowsing, but there is little evidence that it was a great success. Of course if it were such a success, no one would be likely to mention the fact, for gold is gold, even if it lies unused in American vaults. But if it had been a magnificent success, why has no one yet found the treasure of Attila? This prodigious booty, buried after he had had a fit on his wedding night, not his first wedding by any means, was secured by a diversion of the river. That treasure, the loot from most of Europe, must still be there and of incalculable interest to a world thrilled by the discoveries of archaeology. If I were a little less stiff, I would like to try my hand at finding Attila's treasure. This is the period, the Dark Ages, on which I have done most work. It would fascinate me to see what Attila had looted from the late Roman Empire.

But here we come to another interesting matter. Witches, by which are meant those who cast hostile spells against others and not just the devotees of an old religion, are by common belief in the countryside, unable to cross running water. So are ghosts for that matter. If there is anything in the belief, then running water is, like rowan, probably an interrupter.

It is not difficult to test this. Stand on one side of the sink in the kitchen. Put a piece of elder on the opposite side of the sink and test between yourself and it with the short pendulum. At once the pendulum gyrates. The opposition of the elder to an even flow of current is clear. Now turn on the tap so that water runs between you and the elder and test again. The pendulum does not gyrate. The hostility, if it may be so termed, of the elder cannot pass the running water. Presumably this is due to a field of force caused by the friction of the running water against the bottom of the sink, for there is no such interruption with standing water. In any case, if the active malice of magicians can be sent out as a ray between one personal field and another, running water would interrupt it. Of course I do not know whether it really can, but it seems probable that this popular belief originated in some similar kind of experiment. There is something in the idea.

Unfortunately this probably dispels any great hope of finding Attila's treasure by dowsing. If the hoard is still covered by running water, or surrounded by it on an artificial islet, the water would act as an interrupter, so would garnet inlays in the jewels, and the gold fail to register. Still the courses of rivers frequently change and the treasure may now be on dry land. One would have thought that air photographs would give a hint at where Attila's warriors made their artificial cut to divert the river.

This is not really a diversion. I am trying simply to draw attention to the practical side of all this. It is not known where the power comes from to work a pendulum or divining-rod. It is not known where it comes from to enable a shearwater to find its chick, or a fox to find its mate. But the power appears to be undoubtedly there and we can guess that it comes from the life force which makes the universe work. Many peoples of antiquity and some in this country today believed that the power could be generated and harnessed. Highly excitable circular dances were believed to generate the power. Perhaps one might see a comparison here with an electric coil. The power generated by the excitement could be canalized by those who understood the art and they could store it in the fields of stones or trees until they wanted to use it. I do not know whether power can be generated by this means, although everyone now knows of the power of mob hysteria. But we have seen that something from the human field can be fixed for long periods in the fields of various inanimate objects, including bits of stone. We have seen also that two dowsers working two pendulums can apparently produce a much more vigorous effect. These three points, the mob hysteria, the fixing of rates in the fields of inanimate objects and the increase in activity of pendulums when there are more than one of them, certainly point to the possibility that if you had a number of people generating power, you might obtain a great deal of it, and also that you might be able to focus it in the field of an inanimate object. But, although you may be able

94

to collect your power in the field of a given stone, it is not so easy to see how you could draw it out again, or use it if you could. This is beyond any stage in our investigation to which we may have attained. Also investigation with the pendulum does not seem to show that you can impress anything of your own on the field of something which once had a sex rate of its own. Unlike alabaster which, when I have carved it into figures, takes up my rates of sex and thought, rowan when similarly treated accepts neither. It obstinately retains its own sex rate of femininity and nothing else. It is possible that living trees are different. They certainly have very strong fields which are easily detected with a divining-rod. It is not easy to devise an experiment to show whether anything can be impressed on the field of a living tree or not.

However, folk-belief credits trees with having spirits and in some countries it was believed that they could be propitiated and made to work for those who took suitable pains to persuade them to do so. In Germany, for instance, oaks were frequently hammered full of iron nails. I can still remember reading of an oaken statue of Hindenberg being treated in this manner. Until recently too, it was a widespread custom amongst seamen to step a vessel's mast with a coin beneath its foot. This custom is of great age, for when recently a Roman vessel was found in the Thames, a coin of Diocletian was recovered from the mast-step. This was an offering to the spirit of the tree from which the mast was made. A friend has even told me that the death of his father aboard an east coast Scottish boat, was believed by his friends and neighbours to have been directly due to the fact that no coin had been put beneath the heel of the mast. He was struck by lightning. When I bought my last boat some fifteen years ago, the former owner took care to tell me that he had put the traditional coin beneath the mast when he stepped it. There are many similar cases in this country and oaks are not the only trees to be filled with nails.

I do not think that this propitiation of the spirit of the tree is really related to the subject of our inquiry. The masts of most smaller vessels were normally made of pine; although those of big ships were of oak. Pine, according to our table is a male tree and so antagonistic to mankind. To neutralize its malignant effects therefore, in theory, the object placed in the mast-step ought to have been an interrupter, a piece of lead for example. Copper, silver and iron are not interrupters. I think, therefore, that the offerings were simply a bribe to the god to whom the tree was supposed to belong. In the case of oak, the god would be Zeus, or Jupiter for the classical world and Esus for the Celts.

Iron is, in popular belief, one of the most effective charms against hostile magic. So one might infer that the numerous nails hammered into Hindenberg's statue were for his protection and that of the German State. But iron is not an interrupter. Neither was Germany apparently protected by this ritual, for Hitler came to power. Neither copper, nor silver, is an interrupter. These three metals, for no one was likely to put gold beneath the mast of a fishing-boat, seem to be quite out of our protective list. One can only regard them as bribes to the gods when in their normal condition. But with magnetized iron it is a different story.

If you take a silver spoon for instance and tune in on the long pendulum to the 22 inch rate for silver, the pendulum held over the spoon will gyrate. But take a bar magnet and put it down beside the spoon and oscillation begins at once. It is the same if you hold the magnet in your left hand and then transfer it to your right. A bar magnet has exactly the same effect with elder. Iron is an interrupter all right, but only when it is magnetized. Raw iron by itself is no protection against the machinations of evilly disposed persons!

Yet magnetism may be induced in a piece of iron. Blacksmiths' iron is often mildly magnetic. All iron in ancient times was blacksmiths' iron. So there is no reason why some of it should not have been sufficiently magnetic to be an interrupter. Drawn iron wire nails are of course no use. But what about old iron?

I have a large quantity of iron objects here found in the old rubbish dump. The contents of this dump, which I have excavated slowly with a trowel, contain things ranging from a silver farthing of Edward I, to imported German potsherds of the seventeenth century. Iron objects found in this small excavation are therefore of some antiquity. The iron ones are almost completely rusted away and are not worth the trouble and expense of preservation.

I took a handful of this old iron, it was of course all blacksmiths' iron, and tested it with the long pendulum beside a brass ash-tray of which the prevailing rate was that of copper, 30·5 inches. When the pendulum was swung over the ash-tray, it gyrated as it should do. But when I put an old iron ox-shoe beside the ash-tray the gyration changed to an oscillation. The ox-shoe was an interrupter.

It may seem strange that I say ox-shoe, but I have found no horseshoes in this old rubbish heap. Ox-shoes, which look like half a horseshoe, but have a curved piece of iron turned up over one of the ox's hooves, are very common. In the memory of the man who digs for me in the garden here, the next farm, Edge Barton, or farm as it was then called, had three teams of ploughing horses and one of oxen. Ploughing with horses was an innovation in these combes and now has given place to tractors. People in general do not realize how much ploughing was done quite recently by ox-teams. It sounds so primitive. But the replacement of the oxen by horses in many parts of the country is of quite recent date. Some people still maintain that oxen ploughed more evenly than horses.

I am afraid I have digressed again, as I often do when I speak of things which interest me. But I hope it may interest other people also and they may not find it so strange when Kipling speaks of an 'Eight ox plough'. I have never seen an ox-team of more than four myself. When well assorted, an ox-team looks rather beautiful.

Well, I put another iron object down beside the ash-tray. I think it was a round file, but it was hardly more than a rod of rust. Exactly the same thing happened. The rod was an interrupter. Then I took a typical old blacksmith's nail, four-sided in the shank and with a flat pyramidal four-sided head. I gave it the same test as the other bits of iron with the same result and then tested again. Holding it in my left hand until the pendulum gyrated over the brass ash-tray, I then transferred it to my right hand and the gyration instantly stopped, turning into an oscillation. A few more tests made it quite clear that blacksmiths' iron is in quite a different pendulum category to modern iron. It is magnetic and an interrupter. So, although it seemed so improbable that the belief in the protective qualities of iron could have any foundation in fact, it appears that the only iron which could have been used in the old days came into the same category as lead and rowan. It was something which did away with obstructions and let current flow between a human field and the main source of power.

It seems quite fantastic, but listen to this story. One chilly day in the 20's I had to go out to Manae, in the middle of the Fens, because something or other had been found there. Skeletons I think, but I can't remember and it is of no importance. While I was out there the following tale was told to me:

A local farmer had been left without a horsekeeper at a critical time of year. Farm servants were only engaged once a year. The farmer engaged the only man who was free. For a while all went well, but presently the horses began to go sick. Then they recovered. The farmer asked the horsekeeper what had happened. The man said that the horses had been 'overlooked' by a witch. He knew what to do. He found a frog and put it in a bottle. Then he closed all doors and windows in his cottage and sealed them up. He put several iron nails in front of the door and put the bottle with the frog in it on the fire. Soon there was a frenzied knocking at the door. It was the witch praying him to stop her bursting in the bottle. Of course the retort was that the curse must be taken off. And so it was. This was not regarded as the least unusual by the farmer's wife who was Scottish, but it amazed the Fenland farmer.

Manae in winter is low lying, flat and grim. At this time it was quite a business driving out to it from Cambridge. In its relative isolation you could imagine anything being believed out there and almost anything happening. I suppose the Moor of Rannoch in winter, with its black bog pools, snow wreaths and roots of long dead Bronze Age trees, looks more like the gate of hell, but Manae is to my mind more depressing. So it is not

98

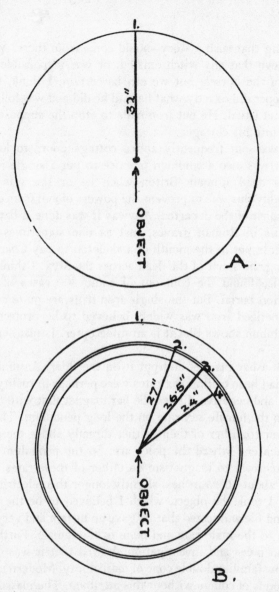

Fig. 16. Pendulum analysis of two pieces of iron. A. Shop-iron, unused wire nail. B. Elizabethan blacksmith's nail. 1. Rate for iron. 2. Thought. 3. Oxygen (rust). 4. Male rate. The rates for the blacksmith's thought and sex have been added to his work. B. (The circles represent the base area of each double cone of the object's field of force)

surprising that such a story should come from there. We need not believe that any witch existed, or was responsible for the illness of the horses, but we can be certain, I think, that the horsekeeper did exactly what he said he did and was following a traditional ritual. He put iron nails to stop the supposed witch getting into his cottage.

Iron was put frequently above cottage doors to keep evil away. It was also a common practice to put a single iron nail beside a dead Romano-Briton when he or she was buried. Presumably this was to prevent the powers of evil from carrying off the spirit of the departed. Anyway it was done. I have found such nails in Roman graves, just as one sometimes finds a bronze coin put in the mouth of a skeleton to pay Charon's fee for taking the spirit of the dead across the Styx. I think I have only twice found the coin out of some 300 cases of Roman inhumation burial. But the single iron nails are quite common. So magnetized iron was widely believed to be protective and the pendulum shows that it is an interrupter. Is magnetism the answer?

I took a bar magnet and put it on the floor. Assuming that what I had been calling sex rates were perhaps in reality simply positive and negative, I tried the bar magnet first with the male and then the female sex rate on the long pendulum. There was no answer to either of them, either directly above the magnet, or at each end where the poles are. So the pendulum did not appear to react to magnetism on either of these rates. It does react to about 20·25 inches, slightly longer than electricity.

Then I took the object, which I believed to be the remains of a round file and tested that. It gave an instant and very strong reaction to the male rate and none to the female. Furthermore it had no poles and investigation showed that it was enclosed in the now familiar double cone of masculinity. Modern machine-made iron is of course without this attribute. The masculinity is induced no doubt on the fields of the iron objects, which he forges, by the blacksmith himself. In medieval times men believed that diseases kept away from the blacksmith's forge. When we look at other interrupters, neither lead nor rowan can be classed as magnetic. In any case the ordinary magnetic field

100

of a bar magnet has never, as far as my slight learning goes, been considered as a double cone, but rather one in a single plane with poles at either end. This is hardly a correct picture. The field must be more like a dumb-bell, but in any case our cones are at right-angles to the ordinary magnetic plane.

Although there are resemblances, it does not in fact seem possible that the pendulum simply reacts to magnetic variations. When I first started to dowse for water with a hazel fork, I thought that it must be reacting to variations in the earth's magnetic field, due to such interruptions in a continuous flow of current as might be caused by a stream of water, or a seam of different rock protruding through a crack in other rocks. Our experiments with the pendulum make this idea seem quite improbable. As far as we know magnetic variation does not exist between two pieces of twig. It seems most improbable that it exists between the cast of the inside of a sea urchin, which died 100 million years ago and a living human being. It seems even less probable that it could indicate sex and thought rates in these long dead fossils. This is nothing really comparable with magnetism as it is understood. Just as you can compare the flow of water through a pipe with the flow of electric current through a wire and yet know that the two flows belong to entirely different subjects; so we must, I believe, assume that the resemblances between our study and magnetism are quite superficial. We are dealing with something distinct and apparently both simpler and more comprehensive.

I think it must be admitted, if we accept any form of dowsing at all, that we are dealing with an unclassified subject. It seems impossible to deny that water can be detected and hidden objects found by dowsing. To do so would simply be obscurantism and laziness. Therefore we must admit that we are dealing with something we do not understand and examine it according to its seemingly strange phenomena. But is there anything very unusual about having to adopt such a course? How would the learned men of the days of Charles II have reacted if they had been told about atoms and the enormous power that could be released by splitting them? They would not have believed a word of it. The scientists of today are very proficient along their own particular lines of study, but only along their particular lines. They are like a row of hurdlers racing. They cannot leave their particular track and jump hurdles on either side of their own. Now it seems that dowsing adds yet another track and it by no means follows that the hurdler on this track will come in last. For the old timers, who did study this subject, maintained that unlimited power could be obtained by it. They may have told the truth.

Chapter Nine

ALTHOUGH many substances figure in antiquity and at the present day as being of supernatural importance, the one above all which comes to mind is salt. There are many perfectly good objective reasons why this should be so. Animals will go miles to 'salt-licks' to get it. It is necessary for the blood, and so on. Of course it makes food taste better. In fact most food without salt tastes incredibly dull, although cats seem to prefer it that way. When you come to the superstitions, the picture is quite bewildering. Salt makes a bond between house-holder and guest, which cannot be broken without loss of honour. It was supposed in India to create a life tie between the giver of the tie and the receiver of the salt. No longer, since the Hitler war, are the Sikhs regarded as the epitome of heroic virtue, because many of them betrayed the British salt and went over to the Japanese. They will probably never recover their status.

Salt was terribly important, but why? Coming back to our own land from those which none of us really understands, we find a variety of apparently absurd conventions. If you spill salt, and this must happen almost every day in most households, it must be thrown over the left shoulder, and then, according to the better informed, it goes into the Devil's eye. In other words, this act wards off evil luck. Why this should be so, I cannot for the moment see; but let us go further. You must not on any account mention salt at sea if you come from the Celtic lands. If you have been born a Sassenach, an Englishman, it does not matter in the least. East Scottish fishing luggers have often been known when out of salt to run alongside an English boat and say something like: 'We are oot of ye ken what, will ye lend us a wee bit?' This seems quite incomprehensible. Why not say that they were out of salt and have done with it? But this not mentioning a name was terribly important. You must not mention your own to strangers, because they might use it to get a magical control over you. There were many things that you must not mention aboard a fishing-boat; hares, pigs, goats, salt and so on. But who would get hold of the names and make evil use of them? To us, sitting beside a twentieth-century fire of a winter evening, it is difficult to guess who or what could make use of them. It sounds utterly and completely ridiculous. Just picture a great Zulu boat (so-called because the design first came out at the time of the Zulu war) slashing up to wind-ward through North Sea spume and when bumping alongside a Lowestoft ketch in a lump of sea, being unable to say what the people aboard wanted, because the word must not be used. Hang it all, the sea is a hard master. The taboo must have been more binding than any of edicts of Holy Church. Have you seen the North Sea in an angry mood? If you have, can you imagine the situation? It appears to be fantastic. Of course the sea is salt, and if you mentioned the name salt inside the boat, the sea might be expected to come in to claim its own. This may be the answer.

Salt appears in old superstition then in a curious double manner. It can bind people together and yet it is unlucky to spill it ashore, or mention its name at sea. It seems to have been regarded as very powerful and yet uncertain in the exercise of its power. It had to be guarded carefully or it might get out of hand and do you harm.

I tested some salt with the long pendulum beside a copper object. The field of the copper was neutralized. Salt is an inter-rupter. Then with the short pendulum, I tested it against my-self. Here the result was unexpected. For a moment or two the pendulum oscillated showing affinity and then suddenly this changed to a violent circular swing. It was more strongly obstructive than elder. I tried salt against rowan. The salt interrupted the rowan. It interrupted the male rate for elder on the long pendulum.

I took a piece of rusted blacksmiths' iron. With the long pendulum it gave reactions at 32, 27, 26·5 and 24 inches, which should be the rates for iron, thought, oxygen in the rust and male rate from the blacksmith. Salt interrupted each of these rates in turn. It also interrupted the rate for lead, 22 inches, and lead interrupted the 22-inch sodium rate in the salt.

This is very remarkable, but the behaviour of graphite, ordinary pencil lead, is more so. Graphite reverses the rate given on the pendulum for sex. It turns female into male and male into female. It will do so for animals and human beings and for the objects, such as pencil drawings, which human beings impress with their sex rates. Further than this, it can over-ride salt as an interrupter.

As I mentioned earlier in this account, I have some skulls of whitings, which are useful for experiments. Some give male rates, others female. A piece of graphite put down beside a male skull at once changes the rate to female and vice versa. Now, if you take a male skull and put salt beside it, you can get no reaction on the pendulum. Masculinity is blotted out. You do not get anything and no reversal of the sex rate. Even the smallest scrap of pencil lead, however, not only gives a marked reaction, but that reaction is on the female rate and not on the male. Graphite completely overcomes salt as an interrupter, and it goes on to reverse the sex rate also. Of all the strange phenomena we have met, this seems to me to be the oddest. Graphite is not lead; although it is spoken of as being lead. It seems to be a semi-vegetable fossil mineral.

As far as I know there are no superstitious beliefs regarding graphite and there is no apparent reason why there should be any. In the ancient world people wrote either on sheets made from papyrus leaves, on vellum, which is made from split skins, or on wax in square wooden tablets with a stylus, a kind of pencil made entirely of hard metal. Sometimes the stylus was pressed so hard into the wax that Latin letters can still be read on wooden tablets dug up today. It was not until the Chinese had invented paper and its use became common for writing letters and for drawing in Europe that a use was found for graphite as a writing material. Before that it may have been a known curiosity, but was not apparently in general use. So unlike salt, iron and so on, superstitions did not grow up around it. Had the ancients discovered its curious property of reversing the sex rate, anything might have happened. It has no sex rate of its own. But I have only to scribble the smallest mark on a piece of paper with a graphite-filled pencil for the pendulum to react strongly not to the male rate, but to the female. Ink, however, gives the expected male rate. Wooden pencils in frequent use have no sex rate from the user. You cannot impress apparently your sex rate on vegetable material, nor on graphite.

It may be important that the rate for graphite is half that of vegetable matter, the first being 10 inches and the second 20. Carbon obtained by burning wood, however, has a rate of 12 inches and diamond, derived from carbon, 24. Since all the other rates appear to have come in some way from changes wrought in vegetable material, it is curious that these rates are not all multiples. Neither is there any relationship to atomic weights. This subject appears to be entirely distinct from other sciences.

All this talk of rates must be very dull to the reader; but there is no other way in which it can be easily expressed. One has to show how one arrives at the conclusions and it is not enough to say that one thing likes, or dislikes, another.

There is another substance which reverses sex rates, for all I know there may be a lot of them. This is elm. Elm is used frequently for floor-boards and if you do not know that peculiarity it can lead to a lot of confusion and mistakes. Elm, unlike graphite, itself reacts to a male rate and it is not an interrupter. So we have a variety of properties which can be possessed by a given substance.

It may have its own rate and interrupt. It may have its own rate and a sex rate and interrupt. It may have a sex rate and reverse, or no sex rate and reverse sex rates. It may neutralize some interrupters. There are many variations. But it does not look as if any of this was due to ordinary magnetism. We do not know what it is, but it vaguely suggests a complication which might be expected of magnetism if it were given the field of another dimension. Let us leave it for the moment and turn to something else.

Why do people, all over the world, spit to avoid evil luck. If someone boasts, they spit, apparently illustrating the line in Kipling: 'Unless ye owe the Fates a jest, be slow to jest with them.' Often that line has come into my head when someone has remarked: 'I will do so and so, and this and that, and then I will be able to do what I want to do.' It has come into my head also at sea: 'We will weather that point on this leg and then we will have a straight run for the . . . anchorage.' I hate to hear it. The wind invariably shifts and one is involved in a laborious and sometimes dangerous series of evolutions. Perhaps the boaster knows subconsciously that the ship will not weather that particular headland, and is voicing the disappointment of the subconscious. I don't know. But to hear boasting makes me uncomfortable and I feel like spitting over the rail. But why should one spit?

Of course I am not in a position to know the answer, but we are collecting evidence which has some bearing on it. For instance, we have found that by using a lock of one of the operator's hair, it is possible to transmit sex rates of long dead fossils from one pendulum to another in a different part of the house. People, who heal with 'The Box', only need to be provided with a spot of blood from their patient, some of his hair, or if that is not available, his spittle. Jesus frequently used his own spittle for healing purposes. The spittle is intimately linked to the person who produces it. We have seen that something of the personality of the operator can be transferred to the things which he makes, or uses. Spittle is clearly more closely connected with the producer's field than some inanimate object. An evil magician is, or was, believed to be able to work hostile magic if he could become possessed of some blood, hair, nails, or spittle of his intended victim. The boaster is obviously giving hostages to fortune by his boast. It would be very rude to say so. Therefore the associate of the boaster must, to protect himself, give something of himself to a protecting power. He spits to give this to Mother Nature, or when at sea to Poseidon himself, who is assumed to be prepared to perform the same function. 'Unless ye owe the Fates a jest, be slow to jest with them.' These words were put by Kipling into Poseidon's

107

mouth, but their equivalent was in the mind of every boatman, or fisherman, who heard such a boast uttered. From time immemorial he had known what to do. He spat over the boat's side, surreptitiously if the boaster was his boss, and so protected himself from what the insulted Fates were undoubtedly preparing to do. Here once again we find a most ancient superstitious rite, which is clearly related to the subject which we are trying to study. Like all the others, it seems absurd at first glance, but, if we are prepared to look at all these things with the mentality of an untaught child, it seems as if there might be something in it. The knowledge of the ancient peoples was not obtained by book learning. It was the cumulative result of generations of observation of cause and effect, handed down by word of mouth. Unnumbered men through thousands of years observed that something almost always went wrong when somebody boasted. Others observed that curious results could be obtained by using portions of the body of a person in a certain way. Others again observed that nature appeared to work in such and such a manner when some action was performed. This was all built up into a code of how to act in a given predicament. And so men spat. Now, knowing what we seem to have been finding out, it looks as if they may not have been such superstitious blockheads after all. We may no longer believe in Poseidon, but the roar of the breakers still reminds us of 'Aum', the voice of God. Again and again we find, contrary to all scientific belief, that there is more in all this than anybody has believed for the last few generations. But this scientific belief is only a very recent skin compared with the vasy body of observation collected throughout the ages which went before. There is no evidence that men are any more intelligent today than they were 10,000 years ago. In fact, from the way they go on, it might be inferred that they are far less intelligent. So it appears that some interest at least should be taken in what was, not long ago, assumed to be proved fact. If you spat, you gave the Great Powers the opportunity and means of protecting you. Who really knows that our ancestors may not have been right? Tonight the south-easterly gale whistles icy cold through every crack in the door, or window, facing its blast. It screams like

108

the Ban Sith, the Banshee. Do I really believe any of this, or do I think that I can show to myself that there is something in it that does not come into scientific curriculum? As I pull my coat collar up around my ear to keep the draught out, I really do not know, and so I go back over what we have been trying to examine. Remember that my baptismal name is Thomas and it was most correctly given. I doubt even my own evidence.

However, there are some things about this pendulum business, which I cannot doubt. I cannot disbelieve it when it produces things from under the ground which I could neither see, nor possibly know about. Therefore I feel I must accept, with great unwillingness, the other information, which it appears to give me. I know well that its information may seem absurd and even totally impossible. But I also see that I do not really know enough about what may be known to a mind, distinct from a brain, to be able to question it. What seems to be shown by the pendulum, as I have said before, is that there is something invisible and intangible attached to our body, which knows far more than we do. I call it a mind, but I might just as well put it in religious terms and call it a spirit. Words are quite useless here. Who knows the difference, if any, between mind and spirit? Both, I think, are quite distinct from brain-activity. At present I am not wise enough to distinguish between mind and spirit. So, for the moment, until something else comes along, I am prepared to think that our bodies, including our brains, are linked by some kind of electro-magnetic field, which I think of as a psyche-field, with something in a higher dimension, which we may style alternatively as mind, or spirit. Furthermore, the evidence appears to show me that earlier men knew far more about all this than we know today.

Of course there are many other superstitious customs which do not fit into this category at all. The full moon must not shine on your face, or you will go mad. This surely because the moon personifies the Great Mother of All and if you do not rise and do obeisance to her when she sails by in the sky, you are being rude and she may well take offence at it. The superstition that you must not see a new moon through glass has become a little distorted. Originally it meant that you must not see it in a looking-glass, for then it would appear to be waning instead of waxing and the fortunes of the viewer would wane also. The similar bad luck implied by seeing the new moon through the branches of a tree was because the moon appeared to be veiling her face from you. But why, when you pick up a cast horseshoe must you throw it over your left shoulder and wish? Why for that matter must you throw spilt salt over your left shoulder, or spit over it to avoid bad luck. All these customs are of course older than Christianity. The reason for throwing things over the left shoulder is the equivalent of persons crossing themselves. You threw it over your heart to show that you really meant it. With salt you threw it to nature to take the force out of any vindictiveness which the salt might feel at your carelessness in spilling such an important substance. The Devil, into whose eye you threw the salt, was the demon who carried out the salt's vengeance. Spitting was much the same. You gave nature something of yourself so that it might protect you from the ill-effects of 'frantic boast and foolish word'. With the cast horseshoe the purpose was similar, but not quite the same. The horseshoe was a lunar symbol of the Great Mother. It had fallen off and been lost and this was unlucky. You had been unfortunate enough to pick up this symbol of ill-luck and thus attach the bad fortunes to yourself. There was only one thing to do. That was to return the symbol at once to nature with a wish for protection and this you did over your heart to show that you really meant it and it was a serious prayer.

All this is perfectly logical if we grant the assumption that the earth is in fact a Great Mother of All and that the moon is her symbol. This is a very old belief and was once held over most of Europe and Asia. It is still held in parts of Britain today and frequently believed in eastern lands. It is a perfectly simple pre-Christian belief. The only way in which it concerns us here is that there appears to be some connexion between many of the phenomena, which we have been studying and the earth's electro-magnetic field. If you are at the stage of evolution in which you find it necessary to represent the forces of nature as gods and goddesses in human form, it is again perfectly logical to picture the earth's electro-magnetic field as a Great Mother

Goddess. Having done so and having, by frequent observation through the ages, obtained evidence that many of the things we have been discussing, do in fact occur, one is more or less compelled to associate them with the activities of this Great Mother. Then, since the Great Mother was one of the two most important Deities of the witches, you are bound to find ill-luck and all the rest of it associated with the activities of these witches. It is as straightforward and simple as that. But the main tenet, as I understand it, of the witches was and still is: 'Do good as you would be done by.' They are liable to be confused in the public mind with Black Magicians and so forth, whose practice is magic and not devotion to some pagan conception of the Deity. A witch has become a term associated more with evil magic than with a religion and this is most confusing to anyone interested. Formal ritual magic is something quite distinct from the witch religion and there is no reason to suppose that the real witch knows anything about ritual magic at all. Her knowledge of magic, if she has any, may be entirely confined to knowing which herbs may be gathered and used for healing purposes. I understand that the nudist games and ritual dances have long been given up by the surviving representatives of the real old witch religion, but that it is remembered that these were once used for the purpose of generating power, something in the manner of our two pendulums and two operators. The ritual magicians did not work in this manner. Naturally the two types of practitioner might at times occur in the same person.

I do not think that I need to say much more here about witches. I do not know from practical experience what they can, or cannot, do. I do know that they believe that their source of power, or energy comes from nature itself, or, as we might put it, from the earth's electro-magnetic field. But there is one well authenticated incident, which as a semi-historian I feel to be significant. When the Spanish Armada came up the Channel in 1588, the Hampshire witches, who like all the others were intensely patriotic, held a great meeting to oppose it. We all know what happened and we also know what Queen Elizabeth had put on the medallions, which she had struck to commemorate this, for Spain, disastrous event. All she said was: 'God blew

111

with His winds and they were scattered.' There was no word about the gallantry of the English ships, many of whom were fitted out at private expense. The wind was clearly the point which struck her so forcibly. It seemed no natural wind from the way it drove the Spaniards right round Scotland and the stragglers back in ignomy to Spain. If there is one thing which the witches were always supposed to be able to do, it was to raise the wind. That is why no woman is supposed to whistle. This is man's magic. He knows, in theory, exactly in which direction to whistle and how hard to do it. I have had pointed out to me from the sea, the place where the last witch was supposed to have lived in Mull and where the last one lived in Skye. On each occasion when I asked why she was noted, I was told that she had raised a storm and drowned some men. In 'Aradia', the witches gospel from Italy, one of the powers that their Goddess Diana was to give to her devotees was to be able to understand the voice of the wind. That is all I know about it and I have no intention of trying to find out more. But I do see that, when we come to look into ancient and obviously pagan superstitions, we frequently find that they appear to be related to this strange subject, which we are trying to study. It seems obvious that there was a great mass of information stored up by the leaders of the pre-Christian religion, which has survived to this day in folk-lore and which in turn appears to be more or less confirmed by the behaviour of the pendulum.

No doubt all this could be taken much further and more significant points noted. But I have not the time to do this. All I want to point out is that in bygone ages men paid much more attention and believed completely in a subject which has been neglected since Victorian scientific ideas obtained control over what should be taught. Now that these ideas are weakening, it is high time that more interest should be aroused in it.

Many of the drugs, which the witches of old extracted from herbs and other natural growth, for the benefit of man, are now being discovered once more. They themselves say that they dare not teach their lore, because so many of the ingredients are poisons if not properly handled. This seems a most sensible reason and one cannot doubt that if they were so foolhardy as to describe their cures to any but the most intelligent medical men, they would be greeted with scorn. Therefore they stay quiet and I have no doubt grin to themselves over the folly of their neighbours, who once persecuted them unmercifully and, as a result, lost much of a healing art, which was both age-old and precious.

Chapter Ten

WHEN I was taught botany more than a generation ago, I was interested in a phenomenon of growing plants, which, if I am not mistaken, was known at that time as heliotropism. Growing plants appeared to be attracted upwards by the sun on one side of their growing point, and so, as the earth revolved on its axis, tended to develop a spiral twist in their stem. Whether this is the complete and correct explanation, I do not know. It sounds reasonable enough; but it has apparently also been successfully demonstrated that growing plants are also affected by the phases of the moon. All old gardeners when I was a boy used to maintain that, if you wanted a crop to grow well upwards, it should be planted when the moon was waxing, and that a root crop should go in when the moon was waning. This, the fruit of centuries of observation, appears to be supported by scientific evidence today, as well it might be. Why should our ancestors, who took more time, interest and pride in what they were doing, have been any less observant than a man in a laboratory brewing poisons to kill off the natural inhabitants of the countryside?

Now, presumably every child is still taught about Newton and his discovery of the law of gravitation, because an apple fell on his head. It is explained that, were it nor for gravitation which causes small objects to be pulled towards a larger one, a force known as centrifugal force would cause all planets to fly outwards into space away from the sun and the moon to fly away from the earth. This state of affairs is often demonstrated by swinging a tennis ball round the teacher's body and then letting go the end of the string. The ball flies outwards from the demonstrator. This illustrates centrifugal force causing the ball to fly outwards, while gravitation is represented by the string. But where is the string in real life? The facts of centrifugal force and gravitation are obviously correct; but how does gravitation act. Surely it cannot act across nothing at all, or why all this weightlessness problem for astronauts in space? Of course we are told it isn't quite nothing at all, but relatively it seems a very poor substitute for the string on the tennis ball, which, compared with the earth, would be many miles thick. Something to the casual observer seems to have been forgotten in this gravitation story, and if anybody can be bothered to think about it and not just swallow everything he is taught, he must see that this is so. No mathematical learning can explain away the absence of the string. Just to say, 'Gravitation sees to that', explains nothing at all. Gravitation must have something on which it can pass. There must be a substitute for the string on the tennis ball.

Of course I haven't the slightest qualification for saying any of these things at all. I am not a mathematician, an astronomer or anyone who is supposed to know about these matters. I am simply a very inquisitive archaeologist. But I am quite unrepentant and do not mind if people say I am daft, for I think I know what the string is. The answer comes from another little ball on a fathom of cotton.

If anyone has followed my somewhat clumsy and incoherent arguments as far as this, they will remember that I said we seemed to learn from the double-cones surrounding every fraction of matter, that they could not easily be traced to their peaks and that it was thought they might be no more than vibrations on a swelling string. I guessed, no more than that, that they were in fact vibrations on taut strings, which were more or less infinite. One end might go down to the centre of the earth and the other go for an unknown distance out into space. This is simply and entirely guess-work. I don't want anybody to think that I know. But to me it seems reasonable from what we have learnt; and I do not see that my reasoning need be any worse than that of trained philosophers and scientists, whose ideas are frequently shown to be wrong. Well then, if you do not

115

think that I have been talking complete balderdash up to this point, look at this. We have evidence produced by the pendulum for an unimaginable number of double cones, terminating as rays, proceeding up into space. These cones interlock and the presumed rays proceeding from the earth must be so close together as to form an almost solid band all round it. It must look far more furry than the skin of a coconut. Out these rays go, fixed at one end in the earth's centre, and, as they are endless, all day long and all night too, most of them end up for a period in the sun. It is rather like the old-fashioned musical box, where the tune is obtained from spikes on a rotating drum lifting up a comb and letting it go again. The earth revolves and the rays are twanged against the sun and against the moon too. At any given time there is a tight band of rays joining the centre of the earth to the sun and another smaller band joining that centre to the moon. Other rays, since all the objects involved are spheres, miss both sun and moon and proceed on into space where a small band will hit this planet or that. But along these bands of rays, when they are in contact with sun, moon, or planets, the gravitational pull can travel, and this is so strong that an object like the moon, which appears so small that you can cover its image with a sixpence held at arm's length, can pull the great oceans up into lumps and cause the tides.

Here I feel must be the missing string to the tennis ball, which makes gravitation reasonable. It would also account for the bending of things like light rays. Nothing would be absolutely straight, except those rays in a dead line between the centre of the earth and the centre of the sun at any given moment. At any one instant there will be one absolutely dead straight ray. Not that this is of much importance.

If there is any sense in this piece of reasoning, we must try to look for evidence with the pendulum. It was in fact such evidence, which set me off on this particular line of thought. I do not usually bother my head with cosmic matters and do not care whether the universe originated in an explosion, or by the collection of minute particles of gases in space. I should not expect either idea to be correct. I really do not believe that the human mind is as yet so far developed as to be able to find the

116

real answer. Our talk is as the chatter of monkeys and we are far too pleased with our own very limited knowledge. What is the value of a doctorate at Oxford, or Cambridge, compared with the awe inspired by the constellation of Orion swinging across the clear night sky?

The pendulum does indeed seem to tell us something, although I have done far too little work with it to have more than a glimmering of what it may mean.

If you take a cone and cut it into sections, as if you were chopping up a German sausage, the ends of each section will be circles and, if you do not get the cuts quite parallel to the base of the cone, they will be ellipses. The way in which I found that the fields around objects were biconical was to put an object on the ground floor and measure its basal circle. Then I went up a known height on to the floor above and measured the circle again. It was smaller than the one on the ground floor. From this you have enough information to draw out a figure and when the sides of this figure are prolonged, it is seen that you are dealing with a conic shape. But, as I have said, it is probable that the apex of that cone continues upwards as a single ray.

Let us go on to the upper floor and plot the circle made on that floor by the ascending cone from an object on the ground floor. Mark this circle with a ring of indicators. Do this again a few hours later and it is clear that the circle on the floor has moved. If this is done several times in the course of the day, there will be that number of overlapping rings of indicators on the floor. It is perfectly clear that the cone is not standing still in one position. The apex, or ray, or whatever it is, is swinging round considerably. In the case of iron, at the height of 50 feet, the swing of the circle, or ellipse, appears to be about a foot in diameter. This is a big swing for the size of the base, which is only 5 feet 4 inches in diameter. (Fig. 17.)

At first I thought this must be similar to the spiral growth of plants and be another case of heliotropism. But I do not think this need be the answer. The apex of the cone is certainly not pointing directly at the sun. But there may be a time element to be considered. If one can also imagine rays as being in the

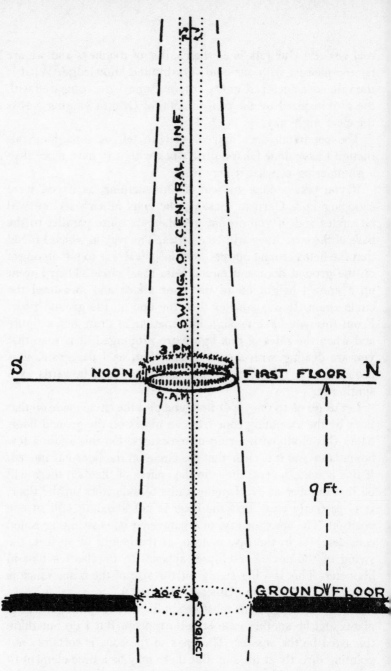

Fig. 17. Simple diagram to illustrate the measured swing of the ascending cone of a copper object. The degree of swing is slightly enlarged. This phenomenon needs much more investigation

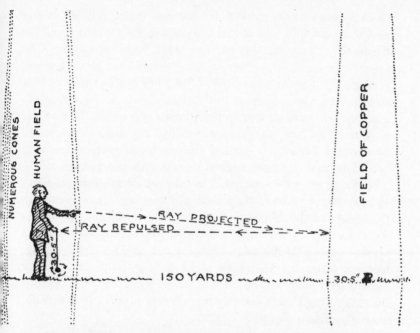

Fig. 18. Diagram to illustrate the apparent behaviour of the long pendulum during distant searching. Nothing really concerns the brain except the tuning in of the pendulum and the observation of its behaviour

nature of filaments, they might bow out considerably between the sun and the earth. Picture, for instance, a small spider on its filament drifting in an autumn breeze. But I am not by any means sure that the movement of these cones is not due to some force from the moon.

However, there is another way of looking at this. We have our own double cones, which may, or may not, be attached to the centre of the earth, or proceed for an unknown distance out into space. But we ourselves appear to be able to extend rays from these cones in other directions. I can, when using the pendulum, pick up the ascending ray from a sheet of iron at 300 yards, or that from a copper pot at 150 yards. (Fig. 18.) There is no reason to suppose that that is anywhere near the limit of such activity. Once again the Manx shearwater and its

I   119

chick comes into the picture. If, as seems most probable, it was tied to its chick by one of these rays, then they must extend for thousands of miles. There is an invisible, intangible, but apparently remorseless link between the mother and chick and presumably it is the same kind of link, which draws the dog-fox to the vixen, the male moth to the female. It is strong enough to alter the whole behaviour of the animals concerned. The people who use 'The Box' do not appear to find any diminution caused by distance between a patient and his blood-spot, or piece of hair. Distance does not seem to come into the picture at all. These rays are extra-spacial. They do not diminish in intensity as they ought to do if they were electro-magnetic waves with the square of the distance. They are something not yet understood. As far as we know a dog-fox might pick up a vixen's call-ray on the Pacific side of Siberia and only be deterred from trotting across to see about it by having some idea that it came from a long way off. One does not know, but it is obvious that migrating birds follow their particular rays, as swallows do, from England to South Africa.

There are swallows which nest in my wood-shed. There are never more than two nests. On a day in April they arrive out of the blue and go straight into the shed and look at their old nests. They do not fly about the district looking for a suitable nesting site. They arrive and fly in at the half-door, which I keep shut all the winter, but open at the time they might be expected to appear. One moment there are no swallows. The next there are two or three fluttering like beautiful butterflies round the old beams in the shed and squeaking with excitement. I feel excited myself, and love to see the little beauties there once more. I do not mind that they are covered with vermin and can seldom cease from scratching themselves. Their nests may be slum dwellings of the most disgraceful kind; but these tiny heroes have flown uncounted miles from the other side of the world to please us with their graceful flight, and of all the possibilities they have chosen our own particular untidy old wood-shed to home on with more accuracy than a rocket fired at the moon. No radar or other electrical device did this. They came straight over land and sea on their own ray, which became attached, like the blacksmith's sex rate when he hammered out a horseshoe, to the nest where they had been reared. (Fig. 19.)

Birds have this faculty highly developed. As a small boy I listened on occasion to the talk of an old ornithologist. He told me of a pair of peregrine falcons, which he kept under observation. While the eggs were being incubated the male falcon, the tiercel, was shot. Within a day the hen bird, the falcon, had called up another mate. Then the falcon was shot. The foster father called up another falcon and the nest went on with a completely fresh pair of birds. He did not know how it was done, but he did observe the fact. I asked him, I remember, where he thought the new birds came from and he replied that he thought there must be a reserve of unmated birds somewhere in the Highlands of Scotland. But the nest was on the south coast of England. Although I have not observed it myself, I have frequently heard of nests being carried on with one new parent. But this is the only case in which I have heard of two. Yet I have not the slightest doubt that this was true. It is just like the story of dog-fox and vixen on a wider scale. The beam was sent out sweeping, in the way I look for things hidden beneath the ground, and 500 or 600 miles away its urgency affected an unmated bird. Of course a peregrine flies fast and when in a real hurry may reach a speed of perhaps 200 miles an hour. On one occasion on the north Gower coast, facing across the salt marshes, a friend and I noticed a peregrine chasing a racing pigeon coming in from the west. A pigeon itself is no mean flyer. Three times, as we had them in view, the peregrine got 100 feet or more above the pigeon, dived, stooped at it and missed. The whole incident only took a minute or so before the birds were out of sight; but after each stoop the peregrine had to put on speed again to overtake the pigeon and gain enough height to dive at it once more.

Estimates of the speed of birds are difficult to obtain. They fly faster than anyone might think. On one occasion I was driving into Cambridge in a friend's car, which was doing 45 miles an hour. Somebody put up a covey of partridges about 100 yards away on our right from a stubble field. They flew across the road close behind us, swung round over the middle of

Fig. 19. The end of the ray. A returning swallow swoops into
the shed at Hole. 24th April 1964

the next field on our left and round again ahead of the car, to settle once more on the original stubble. I do not think that they can have been flying at less than 100 miles an hour and they were not really trying, or they would not have returned to the same field. A peregrine in a hurry must surely go at twice that speed. It would not take more than about three hours for birds to come from Scotland to southern England, if they had an urgent call. The eggs did not get cold.

The speed and beauty of the peregrine are indeed wonderful. Once as a boy I was sent in the snow on a hare-drive at the summit of Dùn da Ghaoithe, the fort of the wind, in Mull. (Fig. 20.) As I was crouching behind a ridge of rock, a peregrine came over just above my head. Its hurrying wings were out of sight before I could turn completely round. None the less the great gyr falcons of Iceland and Greenland are bigger and faster. I am glad to have watched both of them. However, the speed of birds has little to do with this book and I ought not to have let myself wander off; but I know well that some readers will love birds as much as I do and there is no real need for me to apologize.

I have suggested then that we can bend our rays in whatever direction we like. Of course we would not bend the whole ray for I suspect that this is how the life force really reaches us. But we can send out a beam at an angle to the main axis of our body. We do not do this, unless we are experimenting, consciously at all. But it can be done. I have no idea what forces can move up and down these rays, which apparently could form the string to the sun preventing the earth from flying off its course. But they may be very great, far greater in fact than the relatively trivial power, which is at present assumed for the earth's field. I think that it must have been this power which was the object of the practitioners of the old religions to harness. They collected a large number of persons, each with a given capacity for absorbing power from outside. Then they excited them to increase their potential. They did this in prepared places where the collected power could not escape and drift away over the countryside. We still see the remains of some of these places as stone rings, which are often protected today from being destroyed by

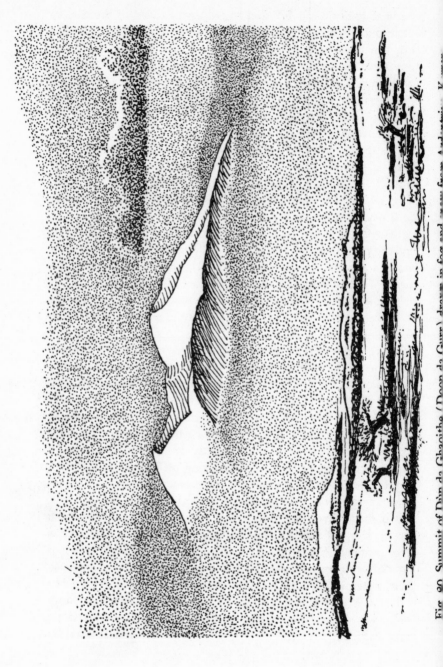

Fig. 80. Summit of Dún de Ghaoithe (Doon de Gurr) drawn in foreground from Ardmeanach, Mull.

an order from the Government. The surrounding stones had been specially prepared for this purpose by having their fields impregnated by the correct magic inductions. Whether it really worked, I have no idea. But I do think that this was the intended purpose of the stone circles, which still survive in many parts of the land. They were laboratories in which power could be collected and stored until such time as it was needed. That is why such intense misfortune was believed to attend those who destroyed a stone circle. They were breaking the ring in which great power was enclosed and everybody who knew wished them ill for doing it. In their inmost hearts they knew this and suffered therefore from psycho-somatic troubles. It was generally believed to be unlucky to move the stones. They defied this superstition, which in some measure they vaguely believed and then they were secretly bothered about it. However, this is an objective view. Who knows how much magic may not also have been involved and what power this may have had? All our research is tending to show that what we know as magic today may well be scientific fact tomorrow.

Chapter Eleven

I THINK I must now begin to collect what we have been trying to study into a composite whole. It is not at all an easy task. If it was any other commonplace subject, like an excavation report, there would be little difficulty about it. But the whole way through what I have been trying to describe, we have been confronted with questions to which no answer is at present known. We are scratching about on the fringes of a subject, whose implications appear to be very great. In fact they seem to go to the root of what life itself may really be. If the pendulum is telling the truth, then we can be quite certain that you will never be able to find out what life is in a laboratory, however many generations you may expend on the quest. For it seems to have another dimension involved in it, which is not concerned with earthly space or time. But all modern science is completely tied to these two factors. If anything is outside their range it cannot in theory occur.

We will fly back in time for a moment. No one is without ancestors who believed that man could draw immeasurable power out of the natural world and they believed that this power could be harnessed for such ends as they felt necessary. We have seen, I hope, because I may have made it neither comprehensible nor plausible, that there appears to be quite a lot of reason for what they believed. In fact, from a Christian point of view, the Founder of this religion was the greatest adept at handling this power of whom we have any record. He could, if we trust the records which seem to be irrefutable, heal any disease, quieten any storm, blast the life of any growing thing, secure a large catch of fish, converse with the spirits of people who were no longer alive and revitalize those who were already dead. But, He always said that this power came from what He called His Father. 'My Father, who dwelleth in Me, He doeth the works.'

This was what He taught His disciples to do and they apparently went out and did it. At times their confidence failed, as well it might, but when they complained: 'Why could not we cast it (a devil) out?' they were chided for lack of faith. They were not apparently ordered to teach a code of moral behaviour. They were told simply to use the power, which their Master had shown them how to handle.

The power was made available by direct contact between Master and disciple. If I am correctly informed by those who make a study of the subject, there was a break in the transmission, the laying on of hands, for some 200 years in the Dark Ages, and so the modern priest has no easy access to the power and at best may discover how to use it for himself. Apparently some do, but not as their right.

Now, whatever you may believe Jesus to have been, it seems that He was perfectly able to handle this power and hand it on to His disciples. It was something which ordinary men could use, if they knew how to use it, and had had the necessary push from the expert. Precisely the same faculty appears to have been handed on to the people we now call witches, not the modern revivalists, but the old ones. They had a Messiah, a female one, who, in Italy at any rate, taught them how to use this power in various ways. They could find hidden treasure, cure diseases, secure success in love, influence the behaviour of the winds, destroy the fertility of man and beast and so on. Aradia was believed to be the child of a god and a goddess, Diana and Lucifer, or Apollo. I do not wish to upset people's beliefs, or interfere in any way with their faith, but I do see a great similarity between the two religions and cannot help thinking that both were once, very long ago, given the correct teaching of how to harness a great power. The account in the Christian Gospels is obviously far more accurate and also probably far more recent than the other. But the devotees of both briefs ought not to have enmity between them. Jesus is reported as saying that He obtained the power from His Father: Aradia as getting it from her mother, Diana. But the point is, what was the power?

Traces of this can be seen surely in what we learn from the pendulum. The blacksmith, apparently miraculously, sets something of his sex and thought in the field of the iron, which he hammers into shape. I seem to do the same with pictures, which I draw, or things that I carve. At one moment they are inanimate matter, soon afterwards they react to thought and sex. It may sound blasphemous to say so, but surely this is a form of creation. The things which we fashion become in a sense alive. We are handling the life force, whatever that may mean.

But this life force also appears to be unfettered by earthly time. Something of it survives and can still be detected in the fossils of sea urchins, which died at least 100 million years ago. We may infer that the life force endures so long as to be virtually immortal. But surely this is what Jesus said of man. It is only recently that people have doubted it. Palaeothic man, some 10,000 years ago, obviously believed that he would live again somewhere. And the bulk of mankind did so until Darwin put forward a theory that upset everything.

Although there was a lot of sense in Darwin's ideas, yet the main theory, seized upon by the careerists of the time and somewhat embroidered, does not make sense if you devote much time to the study of nature. It is just not possible to believe that evolution is an affair of chance. Evolution is obvious; but the cause of it is not.

As children we were very interested in beetles among other things. There are parasitic beetles in the nests of ants and wasps, which differ considerably according to their hosts. We found most of the species in ants' nests, but the wasps' nest beetle was a problem. However we located a wasps' nest—having no other means of doing so we proceeded to assault it as a military operation. Two boys armed with tennis rackets stood with their backs to the nest and hit all homing wasps, while the third poured a jug of supposedly boiling water into the hole. The operation was entirely successful. No one was stung more than twice and the nest was destroyed. In it were all the specimens of the parasitic beetle that we needed.

Now these beetles bear no resemblance to a wasp. They are half the size, flattish and black, red and white. They are only as far as I know found in wasps' nests. Are we really supposed to believe that, through the generations, by a process of trial and error, these beetles changed their shape until they would be suitable inmates for a wasps' nest? What possible inducement was there for them to do so? This kind of situation occurs everywhere in the world of insects, spiders and so on. Every parasite is adapted for its life role and some of these are very complicated. How did the liver-fluke think out an evolution whereby its first host is a small snail which is then eaten by a sheep? These things make no sense as explained by Darwinian evolution; but they are perfectly understandable, if you once postulate an external mind planning them. You can talk as learnedly as you like about the behaviour of genes changing animal forms and perhaps this is how the change is effected. But still you have not answered why it happens. No more you can, because the answer is in another dimension. Some mind outside the time scale prods the genes and can watch it all happening very quickly.

Let us examine the information, which I have been trying to make clear. Just look at the wasps, for instance, which came buzzing out of nowhere towards their nest, till we managed to hit them with tennis rackets. Apparently only returning wasps sting if you are on their line of flight. Now these wasps did not see their nest. They homed on to it on some kind of ray. The privet hawk-moth, in the first chapter, did not apparently see the plate with the rivet in it. It seemed to have come in on a beam sent out by the force of a tiny electric current. The dog-fox cannot see or probably hear the vixen on heat. The Manx shearwater could neither see, nor hear, nor feel by any known method, its chick on the far side of the Atlantic and the swallows in Africa knew unerringly where their own nest was. We ourselves can project a beam for at least 300 yards from our hand and pick up another beam ascending from a sheet of iron. In fact the beams appear to be as limitless as the sex rate of the fossil sea urchins is timeless. If this is not something pertaining to another dimension, what is?

129

However, this dimension includes all the other three. When the geese were migrating above the Canadian airfield, a radar beam—a man-made mechanical affair—upset the fourth-dimensional beam on which they were migrating and brought them to the ground in confusion. The beam, which confused the hawk-moth, was also of this nature; although its mechanical origin was an accident.

When the blacksmith hammers out his iron horseshoe, he does this in three-dimensional time and space; but what he puts into it of thought and sex rates are in the fourth dimension. They are timeless and do not diminish with age. They are probably still there when the horseshoe has entirely rusted into dust.

This is extremely hard to understand and I should not be able to do so at all were it not for what the pendulum has had to say. This I cannot doubt tells us that there is something belonging to us, but not directly pertaining to the body, which knows far more than the brain can learn by making use of its five senses. It knows where things are hidden completely out of sight and what will happen in future time. It is in fact a four-dimensional thing and is I suppose our mind, or, if you like, our spirit.

This mind is linked apparently to our body by an electro-magnetic field and its signals can be recognized as minute electric shocks. Even if there were not a mass of parapsychological data to support the theory, the evidence of the pendulum alone appears to show that this mind must be immortal. Whether there is one mind for one body, or perhaps several bodies to each mind, or a succession of bodies, is not the purpose of this book to consider. Still, as a matter of general interest, I think that the collective evidence suggests that there is one body, while it lasts, for one mind.

We have apparently three distinct parts of our make-up. One we know well, the body. The second is known to exist from scientific study and from the results of dowsing. This is an electro-magnetic field extending beyond the body on all sides. It appears to be biconical and probably continues upwards and downwards for an unknown distance. The third part is called

130

for convenience the mind. Its existence is inferred from reasonable evidence. These three parts correspond exactly with what has been deduced from the study of parapsychology; a study whose respectability has been greatly enhanced of recent years by the studies of that great psychologist, Jung. To the parapsychologist there is the body of course. Then there is an aetheric body, or husk, which is shed with the body when the individual dies. And lastly there is the astral, unfortunate term, body with which the individual proceeds on his next stage of existence.

On the whole this compares reasonably well with theological belief; but it does not seem to correspond exactly. The Church believes in body, soul and spirit. Anyone might think then that this might represent the same idea. However I have asked quite a number of churchmen what they mean by soul and spirit. In sailing-ship parlance, they usually 'fly up into the wind and hang in irons'. They simply do not know the answer. But I have had answers and these, if I understand them correctly, tell one that a spirit is a kind of new blank thing and that a soul is a spirit which has gained experience. This does not seem to fit into the same picture as the other two conceptions. The electro-magnetic field cannot be included in it. One can appreciate that the mind and spirit might be synonyms; but that then a soul is simply a mind with experience. The Church appears to have no knowledge of the all important connecting link, the psyche-field. That this psyche-field is of great importance seems evident. The thoughts in the brain are known to be put in motion by electric currents. The psyche-field is an electro-magnetic one. The impulses appreciated by dowsers are obviously electric ones and one is led to conclude that they come from the mind through the agency of the psyche-field.

Since the pendulum tells us that impressions, which we are calling thought and sex, apparently remain for an inordinate time in fossils, skulls and bodies of insects and, as it is also shown that detached portions of a living organism, such as hair and blood are still linked to the original psyche-field, it seems clear that the field as a whole must endure for a time not less than 100 million years. It is evidently a store of experience

131

as well as a link with such mind as the original animal possessed. Being a link, presumably all this was available to that mind. So, if the parapsychologists are right, when the aetheric body is detached, the new astral body has all that was once experienced by the earthly body at its command. It seems probable that all experience that we have ever had in an earthly life carries on indefinitely as memory. But the astral body, if it is the same thing as a mind, has a much wider range of understanding. It can give hints in a kind of code by the pendulum to its attached body and, in the case of a large number of sensitive persons, it can communicate direct; although they frequently do not understand exactly what it is trying to show them. Such faults as there are may well be due to the functioning of the psyche-field, for this has apparently another duty to perform. If I am thinking correctly, it is the channel by which the life force either descends, or ascends, along the rays extending from either end of the double-cone. In the case of all the animals which we have been considering in this book, rays can also be extended sideways to very great distances.

One can understand that not only are these ascending and descending rays probably channels for the life force, whatever that is, but they may also be channels for the known force of gravitation. This is where the phenomenal powers reported to have been used by historic personages, magicians, witches and so on may lie. It is impossible to doubt that some of these reports are correct. It seems obvious that if you were able to utilize even a small portion of the life force, or of gravitation, the power available to you would be quite astonishing. It appears quite clear that through the ages some people have known how to use it, to the amazement of all who had any contact with the participants in the incident. But we begin to see that this may not be the abnormal. It might be the normal, if the subject were properly studied. If so, it would, for instance, be the end of disease. Although what I am saying may appear to be wild, it is in reality extremely cautious. The start of the utilization of this force has already been made. The Black-Boxes and so on are just the first experiments in this field.

It is because this Black-Box healing is at such an early stage, that there may well be dangers in its use. As long as only one specimen is placed in any one box at any one time, there should be no trouble. But if operators try to save time and employ a battery of boxes to treat several people at once, then all sorts of short circuits and cross currents may occur, through the overlapping of personal fields of force. The pendulum shows that these extend for at least 24 inches for the male sex rate and 29 inches for the trace of gold in a man's blood. Therefore there will be overlapping of the fields of force of two male persons at 57 inches. With females the contact would be stronger at this point. Since two male fields are shown by the pendulum to be in opposition, while male and female fields apparently agree, anything unforeseen may happen if the two machines are placed inside the range of contact. From conversations with some persons who have been treated by the operator of such a battery, it sounds very much as if symptoms may be exchanged between two patients. They complain of feeling as if they had ailments which they never had before. Clearly protection from this must lie either in spacing the machines farther apart than any possible constituent of the patients' fields; or else in devising some form of insulation. The more powerful the machines, the more unfortunate may be the effects of unwise handling. For safety the machines ought to be at least 6 feet apart and this is probably too close. Since the whole fundamental essence of this kind of healing clearly requires the co-operation of two psyche-fields, it seems obvious that there can be no short cut to easy money by operators of batteries. This kind of healing is not like pills, which can be produced chemically of a given size and given strength. It is the employment of force, not yet understood, acting between one human electro-magnetic field and another; neither does it appear to be limited by the bounds of earthly time or space. The operator has to give something from his own field to make it work, because the whole operation is really in another dimension. It is a mental affair and no mechanical gadgets will ever eliminate the field of the operator. Also, since he has to give of his own power to the operation, he is bound to feel tired by so doing. Do not think that I am being blasphemous, but look at what Jesus said when He was touched

133

by the woman with the issue of blood; He said that He knew that virtue, that is power, had gone out of Him. That too should happen to the operator of the Black-Box. To heal, he must give from his own store of power and this is limited. The witches know this too and when they have expended some of their personal store of power, they have to go quietly to nature to get it restored. It is just like a man-made electric battery. If current is used, something must be employed to replace it.

Of course I know very little about all this. I do not know what the power is and no one has yet been able to explain it to me. I call it the life force and suspect that this includes electricity, magnetism, gravitation and some subjects as yet unknown. But, whatever it may be, its employment is something outside our well-known three dimensions and belongs to mind in a fourth.

Chapter Twelve

MORE than 30,000 tides have swept through the Minch since that evening long ago when I looked anxiously over its waters, towards the distant saw of the Outer Islands, hoping to see the green ray. Pulled by the moon, twice a day, the tides flow silently up Loch Snizort and all the much loved inlets of the west. They stir the lugworms in their burrows and wet the feet of the whistling curlews and shrill redshanks. Yet in all these years I have never seen one green ray, nor met anyone who has done so. Instead I seem to have become involved in a maze of invisible rays, numbered by the million.

This is a very difficult picture to appreciate; but, when you see a blanket hanging on a line today, you just say to yourself, 'Oh, a blanket.' You do not pull the thing to pieces in your mind, imagining all the crossing threads of wool which make it. You do not reduce these threads to neutrons and electrons. You seldom picture the sheep from which the wool came, among the heather. You do not even have qualms of conscience about it, as did a Home Guard sergeant of mine, who when asked what had happened to some missing gas-capes, replied, 'I swear I haven't taken them, sir. I haven't taken anything since I sold those blankets to the French girls in the last war.' The object is a blanket and that is that.

It must be something vaguely like a blanket which covers the whole surface of the earth with its invisible rays. We speak of a blanket of fog, so why not a blanket of rays. These rays are not entirely the product of my guesswork based on experiment. Dowsers in aeroplanes have claimed to have been able to locate minerals in the land far below. If, as I think, our cones of force surrounding objects continue outwards and inwards as rays, the outgoing ones must, I think, be limitless in length and so outside our normal earthly three dimensions. For long periods each day, however, enormous numbers of them must be in contact with the sun. Others at given times would be in contact with the moon. Some would contact both spheres. But many others would frequently extend outwards into a void. It would be interesting to know whether the double-cone round an object shrinks when there is no contact with the sun. The taut-string theory might not then apply. This must be a subject of future investigation. The whole idea may well be wrong and the cones produced in some different manner. But if it is partially correct, there might be a very different size of cone when the rays were meeting the moon, and different again if they hit a planet. It is absurd to think that I might get more than a minute fraction of the answers right. I should imagine that a good scientist would feel that he had had a successful life if he solved one of the questions and I am the most unqualified pioneer. I am like an untrained prospector wandering out into an un-surveyed desert to look for gold. If he was a good traveller, the prospector might be able afterwards to draw a very rough map showing where certain springs and mountains lay near the fringes of the desert. Picture him trudging across a sandy waste with his pack and billy-can towards a hazy something in the far distance which may be a range of hills. That is me. Someone else can come later with his motor transport, theodolites and water carriers. But he will not have such an exciting time.

Then too there is this power in living animals of directing the rays. One can prove that this is possible by pointing with one's finger when searching for something. Naturally there must be flexibility in this matter where living and moving animals are concerned. If their fields are to provide channels for the life force, or whatever we are to call it, they cannot be fixed in one plane, or the animal would have a fit when it lay on its side, or ran about. Also our fields are presumably made up of in-numerable cones all interlocking and producing something like a haze round the body. Some of these rays can evidently be pointed at will. But they all appear to be four dimensional. They

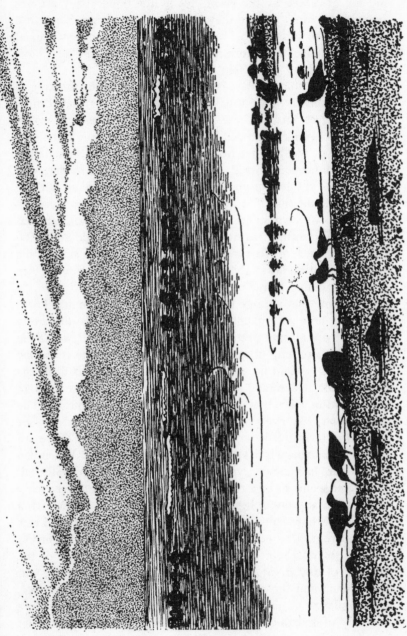

Fig. 21. Flood tide making. The Reef, Benbecula. Drawn after sunset November 1927

are not governed by the brain, but by the mind. They are not bounded by time; nor are they governed by distance. Therefore they are also outside the rules of ordinary three-dimensional science and since all nature is governed by law, new laws have to be worked out to explain their behaviour.

Apparently this is the reason why much religious thinking is clearly in such a pickle today. It is trying to fit a four-dimensional subject into a three-dimensional frame, and is going backwards from its intended line of evolution. It used to be four dimensional, but has listened to so much scientific talk that it has lost confidence in itself. The more it tries to be modern and up to date, the less probable it becomes. Yet I have not the slightest doubt that if it gave up trying to fit phenomena belonging to its own subject into a narrower world and applied itself to a scientific treatment of the other, it would soon discover that much of what it always used to teach was susceptible to real scientific laws. Even in this brief investigation we are surely beginning to realize that.

It is somewhat strange for me to write in this manner. I was trained in an environment in which everything was ultimately derived from an interpretation of Darwin's ideas. I gave little thought to anything of a religious nature. But, if one is trained to reason in a scientific manner, you tend to apply this to things you do not understand. After following out various lines of investigation, all facts seem to point to one main conclusion. The assumption that everything is three dimensional and can be studied in terms of these three dimensions is wrong. There are many phenomena which are outside these dimensions. When you study these phenomena you find that most of them really fall into what seems to be a religious category. It is not necessarily confined to any one religion; but it is something to do with a mind, or perhaps spirit, which is distinct from the body and acts with no regard to earthly time or distance. Its study throws great light on those most well authenticated accounts of the founder of any great religion that we have. If we study our phenomena and those of the actions of this religious founder, the similarity is clear. It is obvious that He had complete mastery of fourth-dimensional knowledge. Further than that

138

I need not go. I regard the Gospels, to a very large extent, as completely accurate, simply because they fit into and agree with a definite line of research. It is surely a pity if the Church of England is giving them up just at a time when it is beginning to be possible to understand them.

There is nothing in the work with the pendulum which most other people cannot do for themselves. There may be a few people who seem unable to use it, but not many. We are not unusually gifted in this way, although now that we are more used to the thing, it may work a little better than it did. We treat it completely casually, but with interest. I rather suspect that any concentration of thought hinders the reaction and that if you really thought hard enough you could make it give faulty answers. In fact somebody else can probably will it to go wrong. But if you take it entirely dispassionately, not caring what the answer may be, then I think anyone can get the same kind of results that we do.

This is a mental business, some kind of coded message from the mind to the brain and the link is very slight. One knows from experience that people in a mentally worried state can cause worry in oneself. One can also prevent this by muttering some rubbish a few times in one's own thinking apparatus. I do not think the link between mind and brain, which the pendulum indicates is any stronger than the telepathic link between oneself and the disturbed person. Therefore I have little doubt that the pendulum's reactions can be upset by excitement on the part of an onlooker and even by the over-keenness of the operator. The proceedings must be coolly dispassionate, really scientific.

However, the interest can be enormous, and it is so ridiculously easy to make the experiments. But the subject is not in the least easy. It is probably more complicated than any other science. Once one has moved beyond the simple analysis of inanimate matter and become involved in the study of the organic, nothing seems to be without its contradictions. The strange interruptive substances, and those which completely reverse rates of what appear to be sex, are most remarkable. Since the pendulum can apparently show exactly where something is going wrong in a person's body, one wonders whether one of these reversing substances could not be used to put it right. What could be done with graphite, for instance, in this way? It might be far easier than any of these Box machines. Men in the Fens used to carry small potatoes in their pockets, because it was believed that they prevented rheumatism. Was this the same principle and did it work? There is much work to be done on all this before even a vague idea of its future possibilities can be obtained. But I feel sure that if one can once link up the fourth-dimensional mind with the third-dimensional brain great advances will be made. This is what Indian philosophers have tried to do for thousands of years; but with a curiously blind eye to the practical possibilities. Eastern ideas appear to be much more selfish than Christian ones. The one aim seems generally the betterment of themselves and not the help which could be given to others. Some of them have appreciated that they were dealing with a great science but at the same time have not treated it in a scientific manner.

This is where I feel we can start with an advantage. The scientific approach is now ingrained in the western mind. Start at the very beginning: 'Strip off the layers,' as Old Sir William Ridgeway used to say, and build everything up from practical experiment in the simplest manner. Bring in no unnecessary complications until the foundations are laid. This we have been trying to do; but it is far too great a work for a single married couple all by themselves in an isolated Devon combe. Still the isolation has a great advantage in itself. You can think clearly without being bothered by aimless tumult and din. For this reason eastern sages frequently retire to caves and so on, far away from the gabble of the towns. There they can not only think in peace, but there is nothing to break the fragile link with the natural rays rising all about them and nothing to cause their own limited supply of power to leak sideways into the diminished stores of other people. When people congregate in large numbers, not only is there a continuous wearing down caused by the noise; but there must be a perpetual sideways leakage, back and forth, to other members of the population, tending to lower them all to the rate of the most nervous and mentally inefficient.

The wreckage from the cities, which washes up here from time to time, shows clearly what is happening. These unfortunates, who would have been bright and intelligent in other circumstances, creep greyly about the house, looking like the 'sad ghosts' of antiquity. Some insulator could probably stop all this and return them to their natural human state. But 'Hurry! Hurry! Hurry!' call the crazy voices and nobody knows what for. To raise the standard of living some people answer. But what use is there in raising the standard of living on some computer scale when no one appears to have the least idea of what to do with life. How can you free people from this terrible vicious circle, when, if you raise the standard of living, they all use their added money to jump into cars and join a mad rush to some place chosen by the leader of their particular herd? Here, taking their noise with them, for they can no longer live without it, they lie in countless thousands, like schools of stranded dolphins, absorbing the same leakages from each other from which they had been suffering before.

There is an answer and it is to find something to isolate each person at will from all the others. Then, perhaps, his or her mind might have a chance to send correct ideas to its attendant body. The link is so weak and the fuss and flapdoodle so strong, but the possibility may be there of finding relief by means of the apparently trivial little pendulum. I cannot be expected to find this on my own. It is surely the business of Church and State and worth far more money in research work than anything that goes towards atomic bombs, or even education. If it is not found, it cannot be long before the whole insane house of cards collapses and the mental homes, already overflowing, will be quite unable to deal with the resulting flood. The answer, I feel sure, is something quite commonplace; but it has to be sought with complete honesty.

What too is this life which we are supposed to live? As far as I can see from the information given by the pendulum, every living thing, or every fragment of a thing once living, whether it is a lump of coal, a fossil, a live cat, or the tooth of a dead fox, has one rate which is common to all life. It is common too to the piece of paper on which I am writing. This rate of 20

141

inches covers the birds of the air and the fishes of the sea, the grass of the field and humanity itself. But the organisms which built up the lump of coal have been what we call dead for perhaps 200 million years. Yet they still retain this rate, which seems as if it must be that of life itself. This life therefore appears to be something to do with the fourth dimension, in which the other three dimensions share. The dead object in the three-dimensional world is still alive in the timeless fourth. If ·I am right in identifying this 20 inch rate with life, and I have no confidence in my own judgement, then all life is timeless and immortal. We have found a rate also for death and sleep of 40 inches. It is apparently stronger than the life rate. But, although it is stronger, yet every fragment of a dead organism still retains the life rate also.

This is something of such very great importance that others must surely wish to take the very little trouble necessary to go through the series of experiments which I have been trying to describe and seek the answer for themselves. This can be an entirely personal search, carrying conviction to the seeker himself without any interference from the opinions of experts who as yet do not exist. If he carries it out successfully he will apparently learn that man can in measure create; although he cannot in the three-dimensional world endow his creations with life. But they are, as has often been said by others in a somewhat different sense, extensions of himself and apparently his link with them lasts for ever. Whether his fourth-dimensional self, which has clearly much greater knowledge than his earthly body, can perhaps make its creations live is another problem. But it seems possible that it might be so. What for instance is this 40 inch death rate, which is double the rate of three dimensional life? Is it not probable that it is the life rate of the higher dimension at a higher rate of vibration?

There I will leave this story and return while I may to the three-dimensional world with the green of the grass and the far off grumble of the sea on the pebble beach; to the buzzards wheeling over the combe and the gulls shouting to each other. All have life in them today in three demensions; but it is becoming clear that although this life may apparently die, yet

142

it remains alive in a fourth. Perhaps I have really seen the green ray after all and been too occupied with trivialities to appreciate what I was looking at. Yes, of course this must be the case, for this morning just as I was finishing this book, I saw the swallows come. At one moment there was no swallow to be seen anywhere. Suddenly some tiny specks swept in from the sea. They raced over the roof of the shed where last year's nests are still on the rafters, passing over the ancient cider apple-tree, which is almost completely hollow and full of water. And then, for an instant, they hung in the air fluttering. They swung round in a swift arc and swooped through the half-door into the shed. They had passed the end of their ray, which stretched from here across Africa, and for a second did not know what had happened. Then they realized that they were home.

Index

145

147